SMOOTHIES FOR BEGINNERS

THE PRACTICAL GUIDE TO MAKE EASY AND TASTY HOMEMADE SMOOTHIES
READY IN A FEW MINUTES
PERFECT TO LOSE WEIGHT, BOOST ENERGY, AND TAKE CARE OF
YOUR HEALTH

ANDREA ALLISON

Copyright Andrea Allison - 2023 -

All rights reserved.

The content contained within this book may not be reproduced, duplicated or transmitted without direct written permission from the author or the publisher.

Under no circumstances will any blame or legal responsibility be held against the publisher, or author, for any damages, reparation, or monetary loss due to the information contained within this book. Either directly or indirectly.

Legal Notice:

This book is copyright protected. This book is only for personal use. You cannot amend, distribute, sell, use, quote or paraphrase any part, or the content within this book, without the consent of the author or publisher.

Disclaimer Notice:

Please note the information contained within this document is for educational and entertainment purposes only. All effort has been executed to present accurate, up to date, and reliable, complete information. No warranties of any kind are declared or implied. Readers acknowledge that the author is not engaging in the rendering of legal, financial, medical or professional advice. The content within this book has been derived from various sources. Please consult a licensed professional before attempting any techniques outlined in this book.

By reading this document, the reader agrees that under no circumstances is the author responsible for any losses, direct or indirect, which are incurred as a result of the use of information contained within this document, including, but not limited to, - errors, omissions, or inaccuracies.

TABLE OF CONTENTS

INTRODUCTION — 6
  THE RISE OF SMOOTHIES IN POPULAR CULTURE — 7
  DIFFERENT KINDS OF SMOOTHIES — 7
  THE POSITIVE EFFECTS OF SMOOTHIES ON ONE'S HEALTH — 8
  FREQUENTLY ASKED QUESTIONS ABOUT SMOOTHIES — 9

CHAPTER 1. GUIDE AND INSTRUMENTATION — 12
  BLENDERS — 12
  DIFFERENT KINDS OF BLENDERS — 12
  STORAGE TIPS — 15
  INGREDIENT SELECTION — 16
  CHOOSING THE INGREDIENTS NEEDED — 16
  ADDITIONAL COMPONENTS — 17
  FIGURING OUT HOW MUCH TO EAT — 17
  SMOOTHIE CUSTOMIZATION — 18
  INCLUDING HEART-HEALTHY FATS — 18
  ADDING PROTEIN POWDER — 18
  HOW TO DETERMINE THE APPROPRIATE LIQUID BASE — 19
  BLENDING TECHNIQUES — 19
  MEASURES TO TAKE BEFORE MAKING YOUR SMOOTHIE — 20

CHAPTER 2. SIMPLE DAILY SMOOTHIES — 24
  THE IMPORTANCE OF SHOPPING LIST — 24
BREAKFAST RECIPES — 26
  BLUEBERRY OATMEAL SMOOTHIE — 27
  PEANUT BUTTER BANANA SMOOTHIE — 27
  CHOCOLATE BANANA ALMOND SMOOTHIE — 28
  STRAWBERRY YOGURT SMOOTHIE — 28
  MANGO PINEAPPLE SMOOTHIE — 29
  APPLE CINNAMON SMOOTHIE — 29
  SPINACH BERRY SMOOTHIE — 30
  PEACH GREEN TEA SMOOTHIE — 30
  CARROT CAKE SMOOTHIE — 31
  CHOCOLATE PEANUT BUTTER CUP SMOOTHIE — 31
  BANANA NUTELLA SMOOTHIE — 32
  RASPBERRY WHITE CHOCOLATE SMOOTHIE — 32
LUNCH RECIPES — 33
  AVOCADO LIME SMOOTHIE — 34
  TOMATO BASIL SMOOTHIE — 34
  GREEK SALAD SMOOTHIE — 35

CHICKEN CAESAR SMOOTHIE	35
SPINACH ARTICHOKE SMOOTHIE	36
BROCCOLI CHEDDAR SMOOTHIE	36
TURKEY CLUB SMOOTHIE	37
BEETROOT APPLE SMOOTHIE	37
ROASTED RED PEPPER SMOOTHIE	38
QUINOA FRUIT SMOOTHIE	38
HUMMUS VEGGIE SMOOTHIE	39
CAPRESE SALAD SMOOTHIE	39
DINNER RECIPES	**40**
MANGO GINGER DIGESTIVE SMOOTHIE	41
LEMON TURMERIC DETOX SMOOTHIE	41
CUCUMBER MINT REFRESH SMOOTHIE	42
SPINACH KALE SUPERFOOD SMOOTHIE	42
PINEAPPLE COCONUT RELAX SMOOTHIE	43
BLUEBERRY LAVENDER CALM SMOOTHIE	43
GINGER PEACH ANTI-INFLAMMATORY SMOOTHIE	44
STRAWBERRY BEET ANTIOXIDANT SMOOTHIE	44
SWEET POTATO PIE SMOOTHIE FOR FALL	45
CREAMY PUMPKIN PIE SMOOTHIE	45
SANGRIA SMOOTHIE FOR PARTY	46
MARGARITA SMOOTHIE FOR PARTY	46
CHAPTER 3. WINTER SMOOTHIES	**47**
APPLE AND CINNAMON WARM WINTER SMOOTHIE	48
APPLE AND GINGER WARM WINTER SMOOTHIE	48
PUMPKIN AND SPICE WARM WINTER SMOOTHIE	49
BANANA AND NUTMEG WARM WINTER SMOOTHIE	49
CHAPTER 4. SMOOTHIES BY AGE	**50**
KID-FRIENDLY BERRY SMOOTHIE	51
CHOCOLATE PEANUT BUTTER SMOOTHIE FOR KIDS	51
SENIOR'S IMMUNITY-BOOSTING SMOOTHIE	52
SENIOR'S ANTI-INFLAMMATORY SMOOTHIE	52
CHAPTER 5. HEALTH AND WELLNESS SMOOTHIES	**53**
GREEN GUT PURIFICATION SMOOTHIE	54
BERRY GUT PURIFICATION SMOOTHIE	54
BERRY BANANA SMOOTHIE FOR BONE HEALTH	55
GREEN SMOOTHIE FOR BONE HEALTH	55
BLUEBERRY BANANA SLIMMING SMOOTHIE	56
GREEN APPLE AND KALE SLIMMING SMOOTHIE	56
GREEN DETOX SMOOTHIE	57
PINEAPPLE TURMERIC DETOX SMOOTHIE	57
BERRY AND OAT SMOOTHIE FOR BLOOD SUGAR REGULATION	58
GREEN SMOOTHIE FOR BLOOD SUGAR REGULATION	58
BEET AND BERRY SMOOTHIE FOR CIRCULATION	59
PINEAPPLE GINGER SMOOTHIE FOR CIRCULATION	59
BLUEBERRY AND AVOCADO SMOOTHIE FOR HORMONE FUNCTION REGULATION	60

BERRY AND FLAXSEED SMOOTHIE FOR HORMONE FUNCTION REGULATION	60
COCONUT WATER AND PINEAPPLE SMOOTHIE	61
WATERMELON AND MINT SMOOTHIE	61
BERRY BLAST SMOOTHIE	62
GREEN GOODNESS SMOOTHIE	62
BERRY AND FLAXSEED SMOOTHIE	63
GREEN TEA AND SOY SMOOTHIE	63
PREGNANCY POWER SMOOTHIE	64
MANGO AND AVOCADO SMOOTHIE	64
PEANUT BUTTER AND BANANA SOY MILK SMOOTHIE	65
BLUEBERRY AND VANILLA SOY MILK SMOOTHIE	65
CHOCOLATE BANANA PROTEIN SMOOTHIE	66
TROPICAL GREEN PROTEIN SMOOTHIE	66
BERRY ACAI SMOOTHIE BOWL	67
TROPICAL GREEN SMOOTHIE BOWL	67
CHOCOLATE AVOCADO SMOOTHIE	68
CITRUS SUNRISE SMOOTHIE	68
GREEN ENERGY SMOOTHIE	69
TROPICAL TURMERIC SMOOTHIE	69
GINGER SPICE SMOOTHIE	70
GREEN IMMUNITY BOOST SMOOTHIE	70
BERRY BEAUTY SMOOTHIE	71
CITRUS GLOW SMOOTHIE	71
BLUEBERRY BRAIN BOOST SMOOTHIE	72
GREEN MENTAL CLARITY SMOOTHIE	72
BANANA BRAIN BOOSTER SMOOTHIE	73
BRAIN POWER SMOOTHIE	73
MANGO GINGER BLISS SMOOTHIE	74
LAVENDER RELAXATION SMOOTHIE	74
PEANUT BUTTER BANANA PROTEIN SMOOTHIE	75
CHOCOLATE BERRY PROTEIN SMOOTHIE	75
CHAPTER 6. FOOD INTOLERANCE AND ALLERGY SMOOTHIES	**76**
BANANA OAT SMOOTHIE	77
BERRY SPINACH SMOOTHIE	77
MANGO COCONUT SMOOTHIE	78
BERRY BANANA SMOOTHIE	78
PEACH GINGER SMOOTHIE	79
BLUEBERRY BANANA SMOOTHIE	79
STRAWBERRY COCONUT SMOOTHIE	80
BERRY NUT SMOOTHIE	80
TROPICAL GREEN SMOOTHIE	81
INDEX OF RECIPES IN ALPHABETICAL ORDER	**83**

INTRODUCTION

Smoothies have emerged as a popular and necessary component of the modern diet. Because they can be prepared quickly, do not require much effort, and include essential nutrients, they are a good choice for people who are constantly on the move. Smoothies are a wonderful way to fuel your body and acquire the required vitamins and minerals that it needs because they contain a blend of nutrient-rich components such as fruits, vegetables, and other nutrient-rich ingredients.

Smoothies are not just a delectable option for breakfast or a snack during the middle of the day; they are also versatile enough to serve as meal replacements, recovery drinks after exercise, or even as a sweet treat. They are also a terrific way to sneak in those vegetables that you might not normally consume during the day, making it simpler to fulfill your daily recommended consumption. There are so many colors, flavors and textures so that all tastes are catered for. Smoothies can be created with a wide variety of ingredients, such as fresh or frozen fruits and vegetables, milk or yogurt, protein powders, nuts and seeds, and sweeteners like honey or agave. Smoothies can also be served with a variety of toppings.

However, because there are so many different recipes for smoothies, it is normal to feel disoriented and not know what to do. This book, titled "Smoothies for Beginners," was written because of this reason. This book is designed to walk you through the fundamentals of making smoothies, from selecting the appropriate ingredients to developing recipes that are both tasty and nutritious. It doesn't matter if you've never made a smoothie before; it will teach you all you need to know. You will be able to make the perfect smoothie every time if you use this book as a guide, and you will be able to begin your road towards a life that is healthier and more full of vitality.

This book will teach you all you need to know about creating smoothies, including which ingredients are the healthiest to use, how to make a smoothie that is nutritionally sound, and how to personalize your smoothie so that it caters to your own tastes and preferences. You will also gain an understanding of the various health advantages associated with consuming smoothies, as well as the various kinds of blenders and mixers that are available, as well as pointers and advice for creating the ideal smoothie each and every time.

Smoothie recipes that are delectable and simple to follow can be found in this book, and they are guaranteed to keep you energized and satisfied all day long. The fact that each recipe provides a list of ingredients, detailed directions, and a breakdown of the smoothie's nutritional value makes it simple to whip up smoothies that are both scrumptious and good for you right in your own kitchen.

The Rise of Smoothies in Popular Culture

Where did the concept of smoothies originate, and what factors contributed to their meteoric rise to prominence in modern culture?

Smoothies may trace their origins all the way back to the early 20th century, when a guy named Julius Freed invented the very first beverage that was similar to a smoothie. In 1926, Freed, who had a juice stand in Los Angeles, began combining fruits and milk to make a drink that he dubbed a "Orange Julius." The drink was thick and creamy, and Freed gave it this name. After the Orange Julius became an instant success, Julius expanded his business to a number of different locations before eventually selling his brand to Dairy Queen in the 1980s.

Julius Freed may have been the first person to produce a drink that was similar to a smoothie, but the smoothie as we know it today didn't come into existence until the 1960s. In the year 1960, a man by the name of Steve Kuhnau was looking for a treatment that would help him with his allergies and stomach issues. He started playing around with blending different fruits and vegetables, and eventually he came up with a beverage that he termed a "Smoothie." After that, in 1973, Kuhnau opened the doors to the very first Smoothie King shop, and since then, the franchise has grown to include more than a thousand sites across the globe.

The 1990s saw the beginning of smoothies' rise to popularity as a health food, and since then, they've established themselves as an indispensable part of popular culture.

As the use of smoothies became more widespread, they eventually made their way into several aspects of popular culture. The decade of the 2000s saw a rise in the popularity of smoothies, which led to their frequent appearances on cookery shows and in celebrity magazines.

Smoothies are now available virtually everywhere, from fast food restaurants and coffee shops to health food stores and juice bars. They are available in an almost infinite number of flavors and varieties, and those who are concerned about their health continue to favor drinking them as a beverage option.

Different Kinds of Smoothies

There is a wide variety of smoothies, each of which has its own flavor character and nutritional composition that is distinctive from the others. The following list includes some of the most common kinds of smoothies:

- *Fruit smoothies*

The most common kind of smoothie is one that is produced by blending yogurt, milk, or juice with fresh or frozen fruit. These smoothies can also be made with fresh juice.

- *Green smoothies*

Produced by combining fruit and other components with dark leafy green vegetables such as spinach, kale, or chard and mixing the resulting product. They are frequently abundant in vitamins and minerals and provide a wonderful opportunity to include more leafy greens in one's diet.

- *Smoothies with protein*

Blending protein powder with either milk, yogurt, or fruit results in the production of these. They are excellent for anyone trying to grow muscle.

- *Cleansing smoothies*

To aid in the process of flushing toxins out of the body, ginger, turmeric, and lemon are included in the formulation of these.

- *Smoothies that can replace your meals*

The purpose of these is to serve as a meal replacement, hence they are produced with a combination of fruits, veggies, protein powder, and healthy fats.

The Positive Effects of Smoothies on One's Health

Depending on the components that go into it, a smoothie can be a source of multiple positive health effects. The following is a list of some of the advantages of drinking smoothies:

- *Digestive health*

When made with high-fiber foods like fruits and vegetables, smoothies can assist improve digestion and promote regularity. This is especially true if the items in the smoothie are blended together.

- *Enhancement of energy*

Because they include a lot of sugar, smoothies can give you a surge of energy in a short amount of time. However, in order to avoid a drop in blood sugar levels, it is essential to counteract this effect with adequate amounts of protein and healthy fats.

- *Hydration*

Drinking water or a smoothie with ingredients that are high in water content, such as watermelon or cucumber, can help you stay hydrated for longer.

- *Skincare*

Smoothies not only leave you with a happy belly, but also with glowing skin, which is something that everyone wants to experience. Smoothies are an excellent source of a variety of beneficial nutrients, which are responsible for making your skin feel and look fantastic. Naturally, different kinds of smoothies produce distinctively different kinds of outcomes. Any alteration in your diet might cause significant shifts in the appearance of your skin.

- *Weight loss*

Smoothies are a useful tool for weight loss since they are low in calories and may be substituted for meals that are higher in calories. For this reason, they are an ideal tool for dieters.

In order to gain a deeper comprehension of the advantages of consuming smoothies, we consulted a number of nutritionists and dietitians for their professional insights.

Smoothies can aid improve digestion, which is one of the key benefits associated with drinking them. According to Kelli McGrane, a registered dietitian and nutritionist, "Smoothies are a great way to get in a lot of fiber which can help support a healthy digestive system." Smoothies can be made using a variety of fruits and vegetables. This is due to the fact that the majority of smoothie recipes call for foods like fruits, vegetables, and leafy greens, all of which are excellent sources of fiber.

Smoothies are an excellent method to improve the amount of fruits and vegetables that you consume on a daily basis, which can help lower the risk of developing chronic diseases. According to Stephanie McKercher, a registered dietitian and nutritionist, "Smoothies are a terrific way to sneak in more fruits and vegetables into your diet. This can help improve your overall food intake and lower your chance of developing chronic diseases including cardiovascular disease or diabetes".

Smoothies, in addition to the nutritional benefits they offer, can also be an effective way to assist raise one's energy levels. Smoothies are a fantastic source of natural energy, as stated by Jenna Gorham, who is a qualified health coach. Because they are so rich in vitamins and minerals, they can aid boost concentration and lessen feelings of exhaustion. This is due to the fact that many different recipes for smoothies include components such as berries, which are strong in antioxidants, and leafy greens, which are rich in vitamins and minerals.

Smoothies have several benefits, one of which is that they can aid in the process of weight loss. According to Emily Kyle, a licensed nutritionist, "Smoothies can be an excellent approach to help weight loss because they are full and they are dense in nutrients". This indicates that you are obtaining a great deal of nourishment while consuming a smaller amount of calories. You may make a smoothie that will keep you full and content for hours if you include things like Greek yogurt, nut butter, and protein powder as some of the ingredients in it.

Last but not least, smoothies are very adaptable and may be customized to match the exact nutritional requirements of each individual. According to Kara Lydon, a registered dietitian and nutritionist, "Smoothies are a terrific way to customize your nutrition. There is a smoothie recipe out there that can satisfy your demands, whether you need additional protein, healthy fats, or fiber". If you look hard enough, you can find it.

Frequently Asked Questions About Smoothies

Because there are so many different kinds and combinations of ingredients, queries concerning smoothies are very common. In this piece, we will address some of the most commonly spoken about aspects of smoothies in order to assist you in making well-informed decisions and gaining the most out of your smoothie experiences.

- *Is drinking smoothies good for me?*

The ingredients that go into a smoothie determine whether or not it can be considered a healthy option. It is essential to use fresh fruits and vegetables and to minimize the amount of added sugars in your smoothie if you want to keep it on the healthy side. The addition of protein powder to your smoothie has the potential to make it more filling and keep you satisfied for a longer period of time.

- *Is it true that drinking smoothies can aid in weight loss?*

Smoothies are an excellent supplement to a weight loss regimen, but on their own, they are not a silver bullet for the problem. In fact, it is necessary to generate a calorie deficit by using more energy than you take in on a daily basis in order to lose a few pounds. It is vital to check portion proportions and avoid adding high-calorie components like ice cream or sweetened syrups while following a plan that restricts calories, since smoothies can be a healthy option as part of a diet as long as certain guidelines are followed.

- *What are some of the more typical ingredients included in smoothies?*

The following are examples of popular components found in smoothies:

Bananas, berries, mangoes, pineapples, and a variety of other fruits.

Vegetables: spinach, kale, cucumber, etc.

Dairy: milk, yogurt, kefir, etc.

Milk derived from plants, such as almond, soy, or coconut, among others.

Spreads made from ground nuts, such as peanut, almond, or cashew.

Whey, plant-based, collagen, and other types of protein powders are all examples.

Sweeteners such as agave, maple syrup, honey, and other similar products.

Seeds such as hemp, chia, and flax, among others.

- *I'd like to make a smoothie, but I was wondering if I could use frozen fruits and vegetables.*

The answer is yes, you can include frozen fruits and vegetables in your smoothies. They are a practical alternative that can assist with keeping your smoothie chilly without the requirement of using ice. It is vital to read the label to ensure that there are no added sugars or preservatives when purchasing frozen fruits and vegetables; nonetheless, frozen fruits and vegetables are typically just as nutritious as fresh ones.

- *What can I add to my smoothie to make it more substantial?*

If you want your smoothie to be more filling and keep you satisfied for a longer period of time, try adding some protein powder, nut butter, or seeds to it. You may also increase the amount of fiber and healthy fats in your smoothie by including oats or avocado. It is essential to keep an eye on portion sizes and to avoid eating an excessive amount of foods that are high in calories.

- *Is it possible for me to prepare smoothies in advance?*

Smoothies can be prepared in advance and kept in the refrigerator for up to 24 hours after they have been made. However, over time, certain components may become wa-

tery or separate from one another. You can avoid this problem by including a thickening ingredient in your smoothie, like as chia seeds, or by storing it in a bottle that has been vacuum-sealed.

- Is it possible that consuming smoothies could put your health in jeopardy?

Even though smoothies could seem like a healthy choice, there are a few potential hazards that you should be aware of. The consumption of an excessive number of smoothies might result in the consumption of an excessive number of calories, which can lead to weight gain. In addition, the sugar content of some smoothies can be rather high, which might result in swings (both up and down) in blood sugar levels. It is essential to pay attention to portion proportions and make intelligent decisions regarding the ingredients.

- Are smoothies a viable alternative to meals?

Smoothies have the potential to stand in for meals and may be prepared in a matter of minutes, making them a practical choice for people who are constantly on the move because of their convenience. Smoothies are a terrific method to get all of the nutrients your body need in a single meal because they may be loaded with a wide variety of fruits, vegetables, and other nutritional components. Smoothies that substitute meals are an efficient strategy for weight loss because they are often low in calories and high in fiber. It is also essential to be mindful of portion sizes and to avoid relying solely on smoothies as a source of nourishment all the time.

- I'd like to add some nutrients to my smoothie. Is that possible?

Smoothies can, in fact, have dietary supplements such as vitamins, minerals, and probiotics added to them. It is essential to have a conversation with your healthcare practitioner prior to introducing dietary supplements to your routine in order to ensure that the supplements will be both beneficial and risk-free for you.

- I don't have a blender; is it possible to prepare a smoothie?

You may make smoothies with a variety of different appliances, the most common of which is a blender. However, you can also use a food processor or an immersion blender. On the other hand, the consistency might not be as smooth as it would be if you used a conventional blender.

- Is it possible to freeze my smoothie?

Smoothies can be stored for up to three months, however the thawing process can result in a change in the consistency of the drink. Pour the smoothie into a container that is safe to put in the freezer, making sure to leave some headspace at the top to allow for expansion. When you are ready to consume it, allow it to defrost in the refrigerator for an entire day.

CHAPTER 1.
GUIDE AND INSTRUMENTATION

Blenders

When it comes to preparing smoothies, soups, sauces, and a broad variety of other dishes, blenders are an indispensable piece of kitchen equipment. Because there are so many distinct models of blenders currently on the market, it can be difficult to choose which one will serve your purposes in the most efficient and effective manner. In this piece, we will discuss the many different kinds of blenders that are typically utilized for the preparation of smoothies, as well as the characteristics that are important to look for when purchasing a blender.

Different kinds of blenders

Immersion blenders, personal blenders, and countertop blenders are the three primary types of blenders that are utilized most frequently while one is in the process of preparing a smoothie.

- *Immersion Blenders*

Immersion blenders are also known as hand blenders, which are similar hand-held machines that are plunged directly into the food or liquid being blended. Countertop blenders tend to be more expensive, whilst these normally cost less and take up less room. Blending small batches of smoothies, soups, sauces, and other meals directly in the pot or bowl is the perfect use for immersion blenders, which are designed for this purpose. They are also fantastic for creating smoothies in individual servings.

One of the most significant benefits of using an immersion blender is the fact that it is simple to clean. The majority of models come with blending wands that can be removed and washed either by hand or in the dishwasher. Immersion blenders are likewise more versatile than those other kinds of blenders.

- *Personal Blenders*

Personal blenders are portable, single-serve blenders that are meant for creating smoothies on the go. These blenders are tiny and only hold one serving at a time. They usually come with a portable cup that may be used as a travel mug and are sold separately. People who wish to create smoothies fast and effortlessly without having to clean a huge blender jar will find that personal blenders are the appropriate appliance for their needs.

The fact that personal blenders are simple to operate is among the most significant benefits that they offer. Additionally, persons who have restricted counter or storage space might benefit greatly from the use of personal blenders.

- *Countertop Blenders*

The most frequent form of blender that is utilized for the preparation of smoothies is the countertop variety. They are available in a range of sizes and pricing points, and they are appropriate for blending huge amounts of smoothies, soups, and other types of foods. Blenders that are designed to be used on a countertop often have a big blending jar that has a capacity of at least 32 ounces, and they are designed to be used on a countertop.

The power of countertop blenders is one of the most significant advantages of these appliances. They often have more power than immersion blenders or personal blenders, and as a result, they are able to quickly blend stubborn items like ice and frozen fruit. In addition, countertop blenders typically come with a number of blending speed settings, allowing you to tailor the blending speed to the requirements of individual ingredients.

When Choosing a Blender, It Is Important to Consider the Following Features

When shopping for a blender, there are a few different aspects to take into consideration, the most important of which are the motor power, the blending speed settings, and the blade design.

- *Motor Power*

The strength of a blender's motor is directly proportional to how well it can process difficult items like ice and frozen fruit. Smoothies can be easily prepared with a blender that has a motor power of at least 500 watts, which is sufficient for typical domestic use. On the other hand, if you intend to combine tougher items such as nuts or seeds, you might want to consider purchasing a blender that has a more powerful engine.

- *Optional Blending Velocities*

When shopping for a blender, you should also give careful consideration to the different blending speeds available. The majority of blenders come with a variety of speed settings, allowing you to tailor the blending speed to the specific needs of the ingredients you're working with. For instance, you might want to begin blending soft fruits at a moderate speed, and then gradually raise the speed as you move on to blending tougher items such as frozen fruit and ice.

- *Blade Design*

The configuration of the blades of a blender can also have an impact on how well it combines different substances. Blenders with two-pronged blades are more suited for mixing soft components such as fruits and vegetables, while blenders with four-pronged blades are often more effective at blending harder ingredients such as ice and frozen fruit.

Another design aspect to consider is the blade material. Blades made of stainless steel are known to have a longer lifespan and greater degree of durability compared to blades made of plastic. They are also more successful at blending components that are difficult to combine. Stainless steel blades, on the other hand, can be significantly more expensive than plastic blades.

Added Advantages and Functions

When choosing a blender, there are a number of other factors to take into consideration. Some blenders come with settings that are pre-programmed for particular kinds of foods, such as those used to make soups, ice cream, and smoothies. Other blenders may have extra functions, such as a pulse button that enables you to combine ingredients in brief bursts for a more exact blend. This feature is available on some models.

When choosing a blender, another important aspect to consider is ease of use and cleaning. Look for a blender that can be put together and taken apart quickly and easily so that it can be cleaned quickly. After creating smoothies, cleaning up can be a breeze if you use a blender that has components that are safe for the dishwasher.

Centrifuges, Extractors, Juicers for Smoothies

Any person who enjoys making smoothies should have appliances such as centrifuges, extractors, and juicers. These machines extract the juice as well as the nutrients from fruits and vegetables, resulting in a beverage that is both delectable and good for you. In this section, we will discuss the distinctions between centrifuges, extractors, and juicers in order to assist you in selecting the machine that will best meet your requirements.

- *Centrifuges:*

The process of extracting juice from fruits and vegetables using centrifugal juicers involves spinning the produce at high speeds. They are equipped with a blade or a series of blades that first shred the produce and then spin it at high speeds in order to separate the juice from the pulp. Juicers that use centrifuges are typically the least expensive and easiest to use of all the available options. They do exceptionally well when it comes to extracting juice from hard fruits and vegetables like apples, carrots, and beets.

During the juicing process, centrifuges can generate heat, which can lower the nutritional value of the juice that is produced. This is one of the disadvantages of using centrifuges. Additionally, in comparison to other types of juicers, they generate a greater amount of foam, which can result in a less smooth end product. On the other hand, a centrifuge is a wonderful alternative if you are searching for a juicer that is not only inexpensive but also simple to use for tough fruits and vegetables.

- *Extractors:*

The process of extracting juice from fruits and vegetables using an extractor, also known as a masticating or cold-press juicer, involves grinding the food very slowly. They crush the fruit and vegetables with a slow but powerful motor and either a screw or an auger to extract the juice. When it comes to extracting juice from leafy greens and other soft fruits and vegetables, extractors are typically more expensive than centrifuges, despite the fact that they are more effective at doing so.

Extractors are characterized by their slow and gentle operation, which allows them to produce significantly less heat and foam than centrifuges. This indicates that the juice they generate has a better nutritional value and a more refined consistency than *juice made from other fruits and vegetables. In addition, extractors are more versatile than centrifuges because they may be used to prepare baby food, nut milk, and soy milk, among other things.*

The disadvantages of extractors include the fact that they are often more expensive than centrifuges and that they might be more challenging to clean. Because they function most effectively with smaller bits of vegetables, they also demand a greater amount of time to prepare. On the other hand, if you want a juicer that is both high-quality and versatile, meaning that it can extract juice from a wide variety of fruits and vegetables, an extractor is a great option.

- *Juicers:*

A smoothie can be made using a special kind of juicer called a smoothie juicer, which is a form of mixer that blends fruits and vegetables with liquid. They normally feature a huge capacity as well as a robust motor so that they can combine even the most difficult substances. If you want to prepare a meal or snack that is simple and fast, purchasing a juicer that can also produce smoothies is a great option.

One of the drawbacks of using juicers to make smoothies is that they do not separate the pulp from the juice. This results in the smoothie having the potential to be more dense and packed with fiber than the juice would. In general, they are not as effective as centrifuges or extractors when it comes to the process of juice extraction. A smoothie juicer, on the other hand, is a wonderful alternative if you're seeking for a way to produce smoothies that is both convenient and delicious.

Storage Tips

These home appliances are not only costly, but they also have certain maintenance and storage requirements that must be met in order to preserve their longevity and achieve their full potential. In this section, we will go over some suggestions for the proper storage of smoothie blenders, centrifuges, extractors, and juicers.

- *Ensure that the appliance is spotless.*

It is essential to completely clean any home appliance before putting it away for storage. This will prevent any food particles from becoming lodged, as well as any mold development that might have occurred. Disassemble the centrifuge, extractor, or juicer, and wash all the removable parts with warm soapy water. This step is necessary for cleaning these types of appliances. To clean any spots that are difficult to access, you should use a brush. Before reassembling the appliance, be sure that all of the components have been washed and completely dried.

- *Keep in a cool, dry place.*

After you have finished cleaning the appliance, check to see that it is totally dry before putting it away. Rust and other forms of corrosion can be caused by dampness, which can result in the appliance being damaged. Put the appliance away in a dry location, far from any sources of moisture or humidity. A cupboard or pantry in the kitchen is an excellent choice.

Additionally, high temperatures pose a threat to the appliance, particularly to the motor. For this reason, it is important to keep the device out of direct sunlight and away from heat sources, such as stoves or ovens. Storing it in a cool environment is recommended. A cabinet or pantry that is situated away from the range or oven is a smart choice.

- *Put away in the appropriate location.*

Ensure that the appliance is stored in the appropriate orientation to avoid causing any harm to the motor or any of the other components. When storing centrifuges, ensure that they are standing upright so that the motor does not become out of alignment. When storing juicers and extractors, it is best to lay them out horizontally so that the weight of the engine does not cause any of the parts to become damaged.

- *Always keep things in their original packaging.*

It is best to keep the appliance in the packaging it came in if at all possible. The appliance will be shielded from damage while being transported and stored thanks to the protective packing. If you do not have the item's original packing, you can substitute a box with padding or a plastic container for storage.

- *Guard the cutting edges.*

If care is not taken when handling the device, the blades on it are extremely sharp and could result in an injury. Before putting the blades away, cover them with a piece of cardboard or a towel to prevent them from getting damaged. Because of this, the blades will not come into contact with any other items, which will keep them from becoming damaged or dull.

- *Utilize a covering.*

If the appliance does not come with a cover, you can cover it with a piece of plastic wrap or a dish towel if it does not have its own cover. By doing this, dust and filth will not be able to accumulate on the appliance.

- *Make consistent use of it.*

Finally, using the appliance on a consistent basis is the most effective approach to preserve it. Home appliances that sit unused for extended periods of time run the risk of developing rust or becoming stiff. Using the appliance on a consistent basis will keep it in good working order and protect it from any damage that could be caused by extended periods of inactivity.

Ingredient Selection

The secret to making a delicious smoothie lies in picking the appropriate components and preparing them in the appropriate manner. This article will discuss the top items that should be used in smoothies, as well as how to properly prepare those ingredients so that they may be blended.

Choosing the Ingredients Needed

The alternatives are virtually limitless once it comes to putting together a smoothie's ingredient list. However, there are a few essential considerations you need to keep in mind if you want to make sure that your smoothie is not only tasty but also nutritious.

- *Fruits and Vegetables*

The base of any good smoothie should be

comprised of both fruit and veggies. They are an excellent source of critical vitamins, minerals, and antioxidants, all of which contribute to the general health of the body. In order to ensure that your smoothie contains a wide variety of nutrients, it is important to use fruits and vegetables that have a variety of hues.

Bananas, mangoes, pineapples, and berries (strawberries, blueberries, and raspberries), to name a few, are among the best fruits for use in making smoothies. Smoothies can also benefit from the addition of vegetables such as spinach, kale, cucumber, and carrots.

Additional Components

There are a wide variety of other components, in addition to fruits and vegetables, that can lend taste to your smoothies in addition to contributing to their nutritional value. The following are some wonderful choices:

1. Protein sources include Greek yogurt, silken tofu, or protein powder
2. Butter made from nuts, avocado, or oil made from coconut are examples of healthy fats.
3. Honey, maple syrup, and dates are examples of naturally occurring sweeteners.
4. Foods that are considered to be superfoods, such as chia seeds, flax seeds, or acai powder

Figuring Out How Much to Eat

To make sure that your smoothie has a good mix of flavors and is not excessively heavy in sugar or calories, you need to make sure that you measure out the proper amount of each ingredient. Utilizing measuring cups or a kitchen scale is an easy and convenient way to accurately measure quantities.

When making smoothies, you should aim for a ratio of approximately 2 cups of fruits and vegetables to 1 cup of liquid (either water, milk, or juice). Add-ins can be included in smaller amounts, often between one and two teaspoons per smoothie. Examples of these include protein powder and nut butter.

- *Preparing Ingredients*

After you have chosen your components and determined how much of each you will need, the next step is to get those ingredients ready to be blended. Preparing ingredients to be blended can be done in a number of different ways, depending on the type of ingredient being used.

- *Fruits and Vegetables*

When making smoothies with fresh fruits and vegetables, it is critical to give them a careful and complete washing before adding them to the blender. Before blending, it is recommended to peel and chop more fibrous fruits and vegetables, such as carrots and apples, into smaller pieces so that they are easier to combine.

It is possible to give your smoothies a creamier consistency by freezing certain fruits, such as bananas, berries, and mangoes, before you add them to the blender. Simply cut the fruit into bite-sized pieces and store them in a jar with a tight-fitting lid in the freezer until you are ready to use them.

- Add-Ins

There is no need to do any preparation before tossing ingredients like protein powder, nut butter, and other add-ins into the blender. If, on the other hand, you intend to use natural sweeteners such as honey or dates, it is possible that you will first need to soften them by soaking them in water for a few minutes before using them.

If you keep these pointers in mind, you'll be well on your way to making smoothies at home that are not only delicious but also beneficial to your health.

Smoothie Customization

The best thing about smoothies is that they can be tailored to your specific dietary requirements and flavor preferences in an almost unlimited number of ways. In this section, we will discuss the several ways in which smoothies can be personalized, including altering the amounts of sweetness, integrating healthy fats, and selecting the appropriate type of liquid base.

- Adjusting Sweetness Levels

Adjusting the amount of sweetness in a smoothie is one of the most straightforward ways to personalize it. Smoothies get their natural sweetness from the fruits that are used to make them, but you can adjust the level of sweetness to suit your taste. Maple syrup, dates or honey are some examples of natural sweeteners that can be used in place of refined sugar to get the desired level of sweetness.

If, on the other hand, you are attempting to cut down on the amount of sugar you consume, you can change the level of sweetness by utilizing fruits that are lower in sugar, such as berries or citrus, or by using unsweetened milk or water as your liquid basis instead of sweetened milk or juice.

Including Heart-Healthy Fats

A well-balanced diet must include healthy fats because they help you feel satisfied for longer and are an essential component of such a diet. Adding some beneficial fats to your smoothie is a simple way to make it more enjoyable and filling after you've finished drinking it.

Nut butter, avocado, chia seeds, flax seeds, and coconut oil are all fantastic additions to smoothies that provide a healthy source of fat. Other alternatives include flax seeds and chia seeds. Your smoothie will have a more creamy consistency thanks to the addition of these components, which also contribute a variety of nutrients and are beneficial to your health in other ways.

Adding Protein Powder

Protein is a vital ingredient that not only assists in the development and repair of muscular tissue but also helps you feel full and pleased throughout the day. Making your smoothie into a complete meal can be as simple as adding a scoop of protein powder to it.

Whey, soy, pea, and collagen protein powders are just some of the various varieties of protein powders that can be purchased today. Pick the option that satisfies both your dietary requirements and your tastes in terms of flavor.

How to Determine the Appropriate Liquid Base

The liquid basis of a smoothie is an essential component because of the impact it has on both the consistency and the taste of the finished product. Milk, juice, water, coconut water, and nut milk are just some of the many various kinds of liquid bases that can be used.

Your smoothie will have a creamier texture if you use milk or nut milk in it, and a more flavorful and sweet taste if you use juice. Your smoothie may benefit from the addition of water, which is low in calories and can help cut down on the amount of sugar it contains. Because it is both hydrating and delivers electrolytes, coconut water is an excellent ingredient to include in smoothies that are intended to be consumed after a workout.

Experimenting with various liquid bases can help you find the ideal combination for satisfying both your tastes in terms of flavor and your requirements in terms of nutrition.

Making Smoothies Tailored to Your Particular Objectives

In addition to the broad guidelines shown here for personalizing smoothies, you can also adjust the ingredients in your drink to achieve certain objectives. Take, for instance:

- After-workout smoothies should include one scoop of protein powder and a liquid base such as coconut water for the purpose of rehydrating the body.
- Smoothies that strengthen the immune system can benefit from the addition of immune-enhancing elements such as ginger, turmeric, and citrus fruits.
- Smoothies for weight loss should be made using fruits that are lower in sugar and bases that are not sweetened. They should also include healthy fats and fiber-rich components like chia seeds and avocado.

By personalizing your smoothie, you can make it conform to your preferences in terms of flavor as well as the nutritional requirements you have. Don't be afraid to try out a variety of ingredients and different combinations before you settle on the best smoothie for your tastes.

Blending Techniques

The first thing you need to do in order to make a delicious smoothie is choose the blending method that works best for you. Both pulsing the blender and continuously blending the ingredients are common practices for producing smoothies.

The blender is turned on and off rapidly during the pulse blending process, which helps to break down the contents without over-blending them. This method is fantastic for ensuring that you have a smooth and creamy texture without having to overprocess the ingredients in order to accomplish this goal.

The process of continually blending entails blending the materials in a steady stream until the required level of smoothness is reached. This method is fantastic for producing smoothies with items that are more *difficult to blend, such as ice or frozen fruit.*

Fixing the Most Frequent Problems with Smoothies

When it comes to creating smoothies, most individuals run into the same problems over and over again. The following is a list of suggestions for resolving these problems:

- Too thick: If the consistency of your smoothie is too thick, consider increasing the amount of liquid you use or cutting back on the amount of fruit or vegetables you put in it. You can also try to thin it down by adding ice cubes or fruit that has been frozen.
- Too watery: If you find that your smoothie is too watery, consider increasing the amount of fruit or vegetables that you use or decreasing the amount of liquid that you put in it. You might also try adding a banana or avocado to it in order to achieve the desired consistency.
- If your smoothie has separated, it may be because you blended it for too long or because the ingredients were not blended well enough. Both of these factors could be to blame. Blend the smoothie once again for a few seconds, or until it reaches the desired consistency of being smooth and creamy.
- Lumps: If you find that your smoothie has lumps, it is possible that the ingredients were not blended thoroughly enough or that there are large bits of fruit or vegetables present. To remedy this situation, simply give the smoothie one more quick whirl in the blender until all of the lumps have disappeared.

Including Ice and Other Frozen Components in the Mix

The addition of ice and frozen items to your smoothie is an excellent method to give it more body and creaminess. On the other hand, working with them might be challenging at times. The following are some suggestions for combining ice and other frozen components into your smoothie:

- Replace whole ice cubes with ice that has been smashed. It will be much simpler for the blender to crush the ice into smaller pieces and incorporate it into the smoothie if you do this.
- Before you put the ingredients in the blender, let frozen fruit or vegetables defrost for a few minutes if you plan on using them. Because of this, the blender will have an easier time reducing the size of the ingredients and incorporating them into the smoothie.
- If you don't have crushed ice, you can use standard ice cubes instead; however, the blending process for the smoothie might need to be extended slightly in order to break up the ice cubes.

Measures to Take Before Making Your Smoothie

You need to have a good understanding of how to properly prepare your components before you can make the ideal smoothie. Before you make smoothies, here are some helpful hints on how to clean, peel, cut, cook, and store the ingredients you will need.

- *Make sure that your ingredients are clean.*

The first thing you need to do in order to get your ingredients ready is to give them a good wash. This is of utmost importance for raw fruits and vegetables, which are notorious for harboring bacteria that is potentially dangerous to humans. To eliminate any dirt, pesticides, or other potential pollutants from your fruits and veggies, give them a quick rinse under running water. You can also use a vegetable brush to exfoliate the skin and remove any dirt or debris that is particularly tenacious. After drying your ingredients with a fresh dish towel, you can proceed to the next step of the recipe.

- *Remove the peels from the fruits and vegetables.*

Before being included to smoothies, several kinds of fruit and vegetables need to have their skins removed. For instance, the skins of citrus fruits like oranges and lemons are naturally bitter, which might have a negative impact on the flavor of your smoothie. In a similar vein, the rough outer covering of certain vegetables, such as carrots and beets, can make it challenging to combine the veggie. Before placing your fruits and veggies inside of your blender, peel them using a sharp vegetable peeler to remove the outer layer of their skins.

- *Reduce the size of your ingredients so they are easier to handle.*

It is essential to cut your ingredients into bits that can be easily handled by the blender before adding them to the mixture. By doing so, you will assist ensure that your blender can combine everything uniformly, so preventing your smoothie from containing any huge pieces. For instance, chop your bananas and apples into little pieces and remove the stems from any strawberries you have before eating them. You can also remove the seeds and pits from fruits like mangoes and avocados before eating them.

- *If it's required, you should cook your ingredients.*

Even though you may eat the vast majority of smoothie components uncooked, there are a few that do require some preparation. Cooking vegetables like sweet potatoes or pumpkin, for instance, makes them simpler to blend by reducing their firmness and making them more pliable. In a similar vein, before to being blended, certain leafy greens, such as spinach and kale, may benefit from being steamed, since this can assist to lessen the bitterness of the leaves. Before adding your ingredients to your blender, make sure they have been properly cooked and let to cool.

- *Freeze your ingredients*

If you prefer your smoothies to be icy and creamy, you might want to consider chilling some of the ingredients ahead of time. Smoothies are made even better with the inclusion of frozen fruits like berries, bananas, and mangoes since these fruits may give the smoothie a creamy texture and cause it to become thicker. If you want to freeze your fruits, you should first cut them *up into pieces and then lay them out on a baking sheet. After they have been frozen, you can then put them away for later use in a freezer bag or another container.*

- *Ensure that your ingredients are stored correctly.*

In conclusion, it is essential to correctly store your components in order to preserve their vibrancy of flavor and degree of freshness. Keep your fruits and vegetables fresh for as long as possible by putting them in the refrigerator after purchase and eating them up quickly. If you are unable to utilize them right away, you might want to think about freezing them for use at a later time. You can also keep your fruits and veggies that have been frozen in containers that are airtight or in freezer bags.

CHAPTER 2.
SIMPLE DAILY SMOOTHIES

The Importance of Shopping List

It is really crucial to have a shopping list prepared in advance that includes all of the required items for your smoothies. In this piece, we will go over some of the most important components that go into making smoothies, as well as where you can purchase them in both traditional and online retail establishments.

- *Fruits:*

Fruits are the first component that need to be included in a good smoothie. Fruits are an excellent source of numerous vitamins and minerals that are necessary for maintaining a healthy body. Bananas, berries, pineapples, and mangoes are some of the most delicious fruits that you can blend together to make a smoothie. Bananas are a wonderful way to get your daily dose of potassium, while berries are loaded with healthy antioxidants. Mangoes and pineapples both have a wealth of vitamins and minerals in their flesh. Your neighborhood grocery stores likely stock a selection of fresh fruits. The produce area of most supermarkets is where customers may discover a broad selection of fruits to choose from. If you want your smoothie to have an amazing flavor, you should look for fruits that are just picked and still ripe. You can also try looking in the frozen food department of the supermarket if you are unable to discover any fresh fruits. The nutrition profile of frozen fruits is identical to that of fresh fruits, and they work wonderfully in smoothies.

- *Vegetables:*

Increasing your daily intake of nutrients can be accomplished in a simple and delicious manner by include vegetables in your smoothie. Spinach, kale, cucumbers, and celery are some of the most nutritious veggies that you may put in your smoothie. Vegetables such as celery and cucumber are excellent sources of hydration, while spinach and kale are rich in iron and minerals. Your neighborhood grocery shop likely carries a selection of fresh vegetables. If you want your smoothie to have a delicious flavor, you should look for vegetables that are both fresh and crisp. You can also try looking in the frozen food department of the supermarket if you are unable to locate any fresh vegetables. The nutritional value of frozen veggies is comparable to that of fresh vegetables, and they are an excellent addition to smoothies.

- *Protein:*

The addition of protein to your smoothie is necessary for the maintenance and development of your muscles. Greek yogurt, almond butter, chia seeds, and protein powder are some of the best sources of pro-

tein for your smoothie. Other good options include protein powder. Greek yogurt is a good source of protein as well as calcium, and almond butter is loaded with protein in addition to the healthful fats that it contains. Chia seeds are packed in protein and omega-3 fatty acids, making them an excellent food source. Those who wish to boost the amount of protein in their smoothies can do so successfully with the addition of protein powder. You should be able to discover sources of protein in your neighborhood food store. Chia seeds may be found in the part devoted to health foods, Greek yogurt can be found in the section devoted to nut butters, and almond butter can be found in the section devoted to nut butters. You can also look for protein powder in the department of the store that is devoted to health foods or to sports nutrition.

- Liquids:

The addition of liquid to your smoothie is really necessary in order to achieve a smooth consistency. Water, milk, coconut water, and almond milk are some of the greatest liquids to add to your smoothie. Other options include coconut water. People who are looking for a smoothie with fewer calories might consider making it with water, while adding milk or almond milk will give it a creamier texture. Those individuals who are looking for a good source of electrolytes and a beverage that effectively hydrates them might consider using coconut water. You should be able to locate liquids in the grocery store in your area. You may get water in the part dedicated to bottled water, milk and almond milk in the section dedicated to dairy products, and coconut water in the section dedicated to juices.

- Sweeteners:

You can add sweeteners to your smoothie if you want a sugary taste to your drinks, especially smoothies. Honey, agave nectar, and maple syrup are three of the most delicious sweeteners that you can incorporate into your smoothie. Your smoothie will benefit from the natural sweetness and delectable flavor of these sweeteners. You should be able to locate sweeteners in your neighborhood grocery store. Honey, agave nectar, and maple syrup can all be found in the health food or baking area of your local grocery store.

- Online Stores:

You can also purchase fresh fruits and vegetables through the internet. There are a number of online grocery companies that provide home delivery of freshly picked produce. Amazon Fresh, Instacart, and FreshDirect are three of the most reputable names among the online retailers who sell fresh produce. You can also get frozen fruits and vegetables on the internet.

You can also identify sources of protein (like Greek yogurt, almond butter, chia seeds, and protein powder), liquids (like water, milk, coconut water, almond milk) and sweeteners (like honey, agave nectar, maple syrup) by searching the internet. These ingredients are easily accessible on Amazon, and Prime members may take use of the company's free shipping offer.

BREAKFAST RECIPES

BLUEBERRY OATMEAL SMOOTHIE

Ingredients

- 1 cup blueberries (fresh or frozen)
- 1 banana
- 1/2 cup rolled oats
- 1/2 cup plain Greek yogurt
- 1/2 cup almond milk
- 1 tablespoon honey (optional)

Directions

1. Combine all ingredients in a blender and blend until smooth.
2. If the consistency is too thick, add more almond milk until it reaches your desired thickness.
3. Pour into a glass and enjoy!

Nutritional value

- Calories: 345
- Fat: 5g
- Carbohydrates: 67g
- Protein: 16g
- Fiber: 10g
- Sugar: 31g

PEANUT BUTTER BANANA SMOOTHIE

Ingredients

- 1 banana
- 1/4 cup peanut butter
- 1/2 cup plain Greek yogurt
- 1/2 cup almond milk
- 1 tablespoon honey (optional)

Directions

1. Combine all ingredients in a blender and blend until smooth.
2. If the consistency is too thick, add more almond milk until it reaches your desired thickness.
3. Pour into a glass and enjoy!

Nutritional value

- Calories: 427
- Fat: 21g
- Carbohydrates: 40g
- Protein: 21g
- Fiber: 5g
- Sugar: 22g

CHOCOLATE BANANA ALMOND SMOOTHIE

INGREDIENTS

- 1 banana
- 1 tablespoon unsweetened cocoa powder
- 1/4 cup almond butter
- 1/2 cup almond milk
- 1/2 cup plain Greek yogurt
- 1 tablespoon honey (optional)

DIRECTIONS

1. Combine all ingredients in a blender and blend until smooth.
2. If the consistency is too thick, add more almond milk until it reaches your desired thickness.
3. Pour into a glass and enjoy!

NUTRITIONAL VALUE

- Calories: 418
- Fat: 23g
- Carbohydrates: 35g
- Protein: 23g
- Fiber: 9g
- Sugar: 16g

STRAWBERRY YOGURT SMOOTHIE

INGREDIENTS

- 1 cup strawberries (fresh or frozen)
- 1/2 cup plain Greek yogurt
- 1/2 cup almond milk
- 1 tablespoon honey (optional)

DIRECTIONS

1. Combine all ingredients in a blender and blend until smooth.
2. If the consistency is too thick, add more almond milk until it reaches your desired thickness.
3. Pour into a glass and enjoy!

NUTRITIONAL VALUE

- Calories: 176
- Fat: 3g
- Carbohydrates: 29g
- Protein: 12g
- Fiber: 3g
- Sugar: 19g

MANGO PINEAPPLE SMOOTHIE

INGREDIENTS

- 1 cup mango (fresh or frozen)
- 1/2 cup pineapple (fresh or frozen)
- 1/2 cup plain Greek yogurt
- 1/2 cup almond milk
- 1 tablespoon honey (optional)

DIRECTIONS

1. Combine all ingredients in a blender and blend until smooth.
2. If the consistency is too thick, add more almond milk until it reaches your desired thickness.
3. Pour into a glass and enjoy!

NUTRITIONAL VALUE

- Calories: 235
- Fat: 3g
- Carbohydrates: 41g
- Protein: 12g
- Fiber: 5g
- Sugar: 31g

APPLE CINNAMON SMOOTHIE

INGREDIENTS

- 1 apple, peeled and diced
- 1/2 cup plain Greek yogurt
- 1/2 cup unsweetened almond milk
- 1 teaspoon honey
- 1/2 teaspoon cinnamon
- 1/2 cup ice

DIRECTIONS

1. Add the diced apple, Greek yogurt, almond milk, honey, cinnamon, and ice to a blender.
2. Blend until smooth and creamy.
3. Pour the smoothie into a glass and enjoy!

NUTRITIONAL INFORMATION

- Calories: 230
- Protein: 14g
- Fat: 4g
- Carbohydrates: 39g
- Fiber: 5g
- Sugar: 27g

SPINACH BERRY SMOOTHIE

Ingredients

- 1 cup spinach
- 1/2 cup frozen mixed berries
- 1/2 banana
- 1/2 cup unsweetened almond milk
- 1/2 cup plain Greek yogurt
- 1 teaspoon honey
- 1/2 cup ice

Directions

1. Add the spinach, mixed berries, banana, almond milk, Greek yogurt, honey, and ice to a blender.
2. Blend until smooth and creamy.
3. Pour the smoothie into a glass and enjoy!

Nutritional Information

- Calories: 220
- Protein: 14g
- Fat: 4g
- Carbohydrates: 36g
- Fiber: 7g
- Sugar: 22g

PEACH GREEN TEA SMOOTHIE

Ingredients

- 1 peach, peeled and diced
- 1/2 cup brewed green tea, cooled
- 1/2 cup unsweetened almond milk
- 1/2 cup plain Greek yogurt
- 1 teaspoon honey
- 1/2 cup ice

Directions

1. Add the diced peach, cooled green tea, almond milk, Greek yogurt, honey, and ice to a blender.
2. Blend until smooth and creamy.
3. Pour the smoothie into a glass and enjoy!

Nutritional Information

- Calories: 200
- Protein: 14g
- Fat: 4g
- Carbohydrates: 32g
- Fiber: 3g
- Sugar: 25g

CARROT CAKE SMOOTHIE

INGREDIENTS

- 1/2 cup grated carrot
- 1/2 banana
- 1/2 cup unsweetened almond milk
- 1/2 cup plain Greek yogurt
- 1 teaspoon honey
- 1/2 teaspoon vanilla extract
- 1/2 teaspoon cinnamon
- 1/2 cup ice

DIRECTIONS

1. Add the grated carrot, banana, almond milk, Greek yogurt, honey, vanilla extract, cinnamon, and ice to a blender.
2. Blend until smooth and creamy.
3. Pour the smoothie into a glass and enjoy!

NUTRITIONAL INFORMATION

- Calories: 200
- Protein: 14g
- Fat: 4g
- Carbohydrates: 31g
- Fiber: 4g
- Sugar: 20g

CHOCOLATE PEANUT BUTTER CUP SMOOTHIE

INGREDIENTS

- 1 banana
- 1 tablespoon natural peanut butter
- 1 tablespoon unsweetened cocoa powder
- 1/2 cup unsweetened almond milk
- 1/2 cup plain Greek yogurt
- 1 teaspoon honey
- 1/2 cup ice

DIRECTIONS

1. Add the banana, peanut butter, cocoa powder, almond milk, Greek yogurt, honey, and ice to a blender.
2. Blend until smooth and creamy.
3. Pour the smoothie into a glass and enjoy!

NUTRITIONAL INFORMATION

- Calories: 280
- Protein: 19g
- Fat: 8g
- Carbohydrates: 36g
- Fiber: 6g
- Sugar: 20g

BANANA NUTELLA SMOOTHIE

Ingredients

- 1 banana
- 1 tablespoon Nutella
- 1/2 cup unsweetened almond milk
- 1/2 cup plain Greek yogurt
- 1 teaspoon honey
- 1/2 teaspoon vanilla extract
- 1/2 cup ice

Directions

1. Add the banana, Nutella, almond milk, Greek yogurt, honey, vanilla extract, and ice to a blender.
2. Blend until smooth and creamy.
3. Pour the smoothie into a glass and enjoy!

Nutritional Information

- Calories: 270
- Protein: 16g
- Fat: 9g
- Carbohydrates: 33g
- Fiber: 3g
- Sugar: 21g

RASPBERRY WHITE CHOCOLATE SMOOTHIE

Ingredients

- 1/2 cup frozen raspberries
- 1/2 cup unsweetened almond milk
- 1/2 cup plain Greek yogurt
- 1 tablespoon white chocolate chips
- 1 teaspoon honey
- 1/2 teaspoon vanilla extract
- 1/2 cup ice

Directions

1. Add the frozen raspberries, almond milk, Greek yogurt, white chocolate chips, honey, vanilla extract, and ice to a blender.
2. Blend until smooth and creamy.
3. Pour the smoothie into a glass and enjoy!

Nutritional Information

- Calories: 220
- Protein: 16g
- Fat: 7g
- Carbohydrates: 26g
- Fiber: 4g
- Sugar: 20g

LUNCH RECIPES

AVOCADO LIME SMOOTHIE

Ingredients

- 1 ripe avocado, pitted and peeled
- 1 banana, peeled
- 1 cup spinach leaves
- 1 lime, juiced
- 1 cup unsweetened almond milk
- 1 tablespoon honey (optional)

Directions

1. Add all ingredients to a blender and blend until smooth.
2. If the smoothie is too thick, add more almond milk as needed to thin it out.
3. Pour into glasses and serve immediately.

Nutritional Information

- Calories: 298
- Protein: 4g
- Fat: 20g
- Carbohydrates: 32g
- Fiber: 11g
- Sugar: 14g
- Sodium: 175mg

TOMATO BASIL SMOOTHIE

Ingredients

- 2 medium tomatoes, chopped
- 1 cup basil leaves, packed
- 1 small cucumber, chopped
- 1/2 lemon, juiced
- 1/2 teaspoon salt
- 1/4 teaspoon black pepper
- 1 cup unsweetened almond milk
- 1/2 cup ice cubes

Directions

1. Add all ingredients to a blender and blend until smooth.
2. If the smoothie is too thick, add more almond milk as needed to thin it out.
3. Pour into glasses and serve immediately.

Nutritional Information

- Calories: 87
- Protein: 3g
- Fat: 4g
- Carbohydrates: 13g
- Fiber: 4g
- Sugar: 6g
- Sodium: 606mg

GREEK SALAD SMOOTHIE

Ingredients

- 1 cup cherry tomatoes
- 1/2 cup cucumber, chopped
- 1/4 cup red onion, chopped
- 1/4 cup feta cheese, crumbled
- 1/4 cup black olives
- 1/4 cup fresh parsley, chopped
- 1/4 cup fresh mint, chopped
- 1 lemon, juiced
- 1/2 teaspoon salt
- 1/4 teaspoon black pepper
- 1 cup unsweetened almond milk
- 1/2 cup ice cubes

Directions

1. Add all ingredients to a blender and blend until smooth.
2. If the smoothie is too thick, add more almond milk as needed to thin it out.
3. Pour into glasses and serve immediately.

Nutritional Information

- Calories: 159
- Protein: 6g
- Fat: 10g
- Carbohydrates: 13g
- Fiber: 5g
- Sugar: 5g
- Sodium: 619mg

CHICKEN CAESAR SMOOTHIE

Ingredients

- 1 cup cooked chicken breast, chopped
- 1/2 cup plain Greek yogurt
- 1/4 cup Parmesan cheese, grated
- 1/4 cup fresh parsley, chopped
- 1/4 cup fresh lemon juice
- 1 garlic clove, minced
- 1/2 teaspoon salt
- 1/4 teaspoon black pepper
- 1 cup unsweetened almond milk
- 1/2 cup ice cubes

Directions

1. Add all ingredients to a blender and blend until smooth.
2. If the smoothie is too thick, add more almond milk as needed to thin it out.
3. Pour into glasses and serve immediately.

Nutritional Information

- Calories: 246
- Protein: 36g
- Fat: 8g
- Carbohydrates: 10g
- Fiber: 1g
- Sugar: 4g
- Sodium

SPINACH ARTICHOKE SMOOTHIE

INGREDIENTS

- 1 cup fresh spinach leaves
- 1 cup artichoke hearts, drained and rinsed
- 1/2 cup plain Greek yogurt
- 1/4 cup grated Parmesan cheese
- 1 garlic clove, minced
- 1/4 teaspoon black pepper
- 1 cup unsweetened almond milk
- 1/2 cup ice cubes

DIRECTIONS

1. Add all ingredients to a blender and blend until smooth.
2. If the smoothie is too thick, add more almond milk as needed to thin it out.
3. Pour into glasses and serve immediately.

NUTRITIONAL INFORMATION

- Calories: 157
- Protein: 13g
- Fat: 7g
- Carbohydrates: 13g
- Fiber: 5g
- Sugar: 3g
- Sodium: 526mg

BROCCOLI CHEDDAR SMOOTHIE

INGREDIENTS

- 1 cup broccoli florets, steamed
- 1/2 cup cheddar cheese, grated
- 1/2 avocado, pitted and peeled
- 1/4 cup plain Greek yogurt
- 1/4 cup fresh parsley, chopped
- 1 garlic clove, minced
- 1/2 teaspoon salt
- 1/4 teaspoon black pepper
- 1 cup unsweetened almond milk
- 1/2 cup ice cubes

DIRECTIONS

1. Add all ingredients to a blender and blend until smooth.
2. If the smoothie is too thick, add more almond milk as needed to thin it out.
3. Pour into glasses and serve immediately.

NUTRITIONAL INFORMATION

- Calories: 278
- Protein: 15g
- Fat: 21g
- Carbohydrates: 12g
- Fiber: 6g
- Sugar: 3g
- Sodium: 661mg

TURKEY CLUB SMOOTHIE

INGREDIENTS

- 1 cup cooked turkey breast, chopped
- 1/2 cup cooked bacon, chopped
- 1/2 avocado, pitted and peeled
- 1/4 cup plain Greek yogurt
- 1/4 cup cherry tomatoes, halved
- 1/4 cup fresh parsley, chopped
- 1/4 teaspoon black pepper
- 1 cup unsweetened almond milk
- 1/2 cup ice cubes

DIRECTIONS

1. Add all ingredients to a blender and blend until smooth.
2. If the smoothie is too thick, add more almond milk as needed to thin it out.
3. Pour into glasses and serve immediately.

NUTRITIONAL INFORMATION

- Calories: 345
- Protein: 31g
- Fat: 22g
- Carbohydrates: 8g
- Fiber: 3g
- Sugar: 2g
- Sodium: 630mg

BEETROOT APPLE SMOOTHIE

INGREDIENTS

- 1 medium beetroot, peeled and chopped
- 1 medium apple, cored and chopped
- 1/2 lemon, juiced
- 1 tablespoon honey
- 1/4 teaspoon ground cinnamon
- 1 cup unsweetened almond milk
- 1/2 cup ice cubes

DIRECTIONS

1. Add all ingredients to a blender and blend until smooth.
2. If the smoothie is too thick, add more almond milk as needed to thin it out.
3. Pour into glasses and serve immediately.

NUTRITIONAL INFORMATION

- Calories: 137
- Protein: 2g
- Fat: 3g
- Carbohydrates: 27g
- Fiber: 5g
- Sugar: 20g
- Sodium: 147mg

ROASTED RED PEPPER SMOOTHIE

INGREDIENTS

- 1 large roasted red pepper, chopped
- 1/2 cup plain Greek yogurt
- 1/4 cup fresh parsley, chopped
- 1 garlic clove, minced
- 1/2 teaspoon salt
- 1/4 teaspoon black pepper
- 1 cup unsweetened almond milk
- 1/2 cup ice cubes

DIRECTIONS

1. Add all ingredients to a blender and blend until smooth
2. If the smoothie is too thick, add more almond milk as needed to thin it out.
3. Pour into glasses and serve immediately.

NUTRITIONAL INFORMATION

- Calories: 110
- Protein: 9g
- Fat: 6g
- Carbohydrates: 6g
- Fiber: 1g
- Sugar: 4g

QUINOA FRUIT SMOOTHIE

INGREDIENTS

- 1/2 cup cooked quinoa
- 1/2 cup mixed frozen berries
- 1/2 banana, peeled
- 1/2 cup unsweetened almond milk
- 1/4 cup plain Greek yogurt
- 1 tablespoon honey
- 1/2 teaspoon vanilla extract
- 1/2 cup ice cubes

DIRECTIONS

1. Add all ingredients to a blender and blend until smooth.
2. If the smoothie is too thick, add more almond milk as needed to thin it out.
3. Pour into glasses and serve immediately.

NUTRITIONAL INFORMATION

- Calories: 211
- Protein: 8g
- Fat: 4g
- Carbohydrates: 39g
- Fiber: 6g
- Sugar: 19g
- Sodium: 84mg

HUMMUS VEGGIE SMOOTHIE

INGREDIENTS

- 1/2 cup hummus
- 1/2 cup baby carrots
- 1/2 cup cucumber, peeled and chopped
- 1/4 cup fresh parsley, chopped
- 1/2 lemon, juiced
- 1/2 teaspoon cumin
- 1/4 teaspoon salt
- 1/4 teaspoon black pepper
- 1 cup unsweetened almond milk
- 1/2 cup ice cubes

DIRECTIONS

1. Add all ingredients to a blender and blend until smooth.
2. If the smoothie is too thick, add more almond milk as needed to thin it out.
3. Pour into glasses and serve immediately.

NUTRITIONAL INFORMATION

- Calories: 221
- Protein: 8g
- Fat: 14g
- Carbohydrates: 16g
- Fiber: 6g
- Sugar: 4g
- Sodium: 753mg

CAPRESE SALAD SMOOTHIE

INGREDIENTS

- 1 cup cherry tomatoes
- 1/2 cup fresh basil leaves
- 1/2 cup fresh spinach leaves
- 1/2 avocado, pitted and peeled
- 1/4 cup fresh mozzarella, chopped
- 1 garlic clove, minced
- 1/2 teaspoon salt
- 1/4 teaspoon black pepper
- 1 cup unsweetened almond milk
- 1/2 cup ice cubes

DIRECTIONS

1. Add all ingredients to a blender and blend until smooth.
2. If the smoothie is too thick, add more almond milk as needed to thin it out.
3. Pour into glasses and serve immediately.

NUTRITIONAL INFORMATION

- Calories: 226
- Protein: 9g
- Fat: 18g
- Carbohydrates: 10g
- Fiber: 6g
- Sugar: 2g
- Sodium: 564mg

DINNER RECIPES

MANGO GINGER DIGESTIVE SMOOTHIE

INGREDIENTS

- 1 cup frozen mango chunks
- 1 banana
- 1-inch piece of fresh ginger
- 1/2 cup plain Greek yogurt
- 1/2 cup almond milk
- 1 teaspoon honey
- Ice (optional)

DIRECTIONS

1. Add all ingredients to a blender and blend until smooth.
2. If desired, add ice and blend again until desired consistency is reached.
3. Pour into a glass and enjoy!

NUTRITIONAL VALUE:

- Calories: 269
- Protein: 13g
- Fat: 4g
- Carbohydrates: 50g
- Fiber: 5g
- Sugar: 37g

LEMON TURMERIC DETOX SMOOTHIE

INGREDIENTS

- 1 banana
- 1/2 lemon, juiced
- 1 teaspoon turmeric
- 1 teaspoon grated fresh ginger
- 1/2 cup plain Greek yogurt
- 1/2 cup almond milk
- 1 teaspoon honey
- Ice (optional)

DIRECTIONS

1. Add all ingredients to a blender and blend until smooth.
2. If desired, add ice and blend again until desired consistency is reached.
3. Pour into a glass and enjoy!

NUTRITIONAL VALUE:

- Calories: 237
- Protein: 13g
- Fat: 3g
- Carbohydrates: 44g
- Fiber: 4g
- Sugar: 25g

CUCUMBER MINT REFRESH SMOOTHIE

INGREDIENTS

- 1 cup chopped cucumber
- 1/2 cup chopped fresh mint
- 1/2 lime, juiced
- 1 tablespoon honey
- 1/2 cup plain Greek yogurt
- 1/2 cup almond milk
- Ice (optional)

DIRECTIONS

1. Add all ingredients to a blender and blend until smooth.
2. If desired, add ice and blend again until desired consistency is reached.
3. Pour into a glass and enjoy!

NUTRITIONAL VALUE:

- Calories: 139
- Protein: 8g
- Fat: 2g
- Carbohydrates: 22g
- Fiber: 2g
- Sugar: 17g

SPINACH KALE SUPERFOOD SMOOTHIE

INGREDIENTS

- 1 cup packed spinach leaves
- 1 cup packed kale leaves
- 1 banana
- 1/2 cup frozen blueberries
- 1/2 cup plain Greek yogurt
- 1/2 cup almond milk
- 1 teaspoon honey
- Ice (optional)

DIRECTIONS

1. Add all ingredients to a blender and blend until smooth.
2. If desired, add ice and blend again until desired consistency is reached.
3. Pour into a glass and enjoy!

NUTRITIONAL VALUE:

- Calories: 224
- Protein: 15g
- Fat: 3g
- Carbohydrates: 40g
- Fiber: 8g
- Sugar: 21g

PINEAPPLE COCONUT RELAX SMOOTHIE

INGREDIENTS

- 1 cup chopped fresh pineapple
- 1 banana
- 1/2 cup coconut milk
- 1/2 cup plain Greek yogurt
- 1 teaspoon honey
- Ice (optional)

DIRECTIONS

1. Add all ingredients to a blender and blend until smooth.
2. If desired, add ice and blend again until desired consistency is reached.
3. Pour into a glass and enjoy!

NUTRITIONAL VALUE:

- Calories: 297
- Protein: 12g
- Fat: 10g
- Carbohydrates: 44g
- Fiber: 4g
- Sugar: 29g

BLUEBERRY LAVENDER CALM SMOOTHIE

INGREDIENTS

- 1 cup frozen blueberries
- 1/2 cup plain Greek yogurt
- 1/2 cup almond milk
- 1 teaspoon honey
- 1 teaspoon dried lavender
- Ice (optional)

DIRECTIONS

- Add all ingredients to a blender and blend until smooth.
- If desired, add ice and blend again until desired consistency is reached.
- Pour into a glass and enjoy!

NUTRITIONAL VALUE:

- Calories: 199
- Protein: 13g
- Fat: 3g
- Carbohydrates: 35g
- Fiber: 6g
- Sugar: 24g

GINGER PEACH ANTI-INFLAMMATORY SMOOTHIE

INGREDIENTS

- 1 cup frozen peaches
- 1 banana
- 1-inch piece of fresh ginger
- 1/2 cup plain Greek yogurt
- 1/2 cup almond milk
- 1 teaspoon honey
- Ice (optional)

DIRECTIONS

1. Add all ingredients to a blender and blend until smooth.
2. If desired, add ice and blend again until desired consistency is reached.
3. Pour into a glass and enjoy!

NUTRITIONAL VALUE:

- Calories: 236
- Protein: 13g
- Fat: 3g
- Carbohydrates: 44g
- Fiber: 5g
- Sugar: 29g

STRAWBERRY BEET ANTIOXIDANT SMOOTHIE

INGREDIENTS

- 1 cup chopped beets (cooked and cooled)
- 1 cup frozen strawberries
- 1/2 cup plain Greek yogurt
- 1/2 cup almond milk
- 1 teaspoon honey
- Ice (optional)

DIRECTIONS

1. Add all ingredients to a blender and blend until smooth.
2. If desired, add ice and blend again until desired consistency is reached.
3. Pour into a glass and enjoy!

NUTRITIONAL VALUE:

- Calories: 209
- Protein: 14g
- Fat: 3g
- Carbohydrates: 37g
- Fiber: 9g
- Sugar: 25g

SWEET POTATO PIE SMOOTHIE FOR FALL

INGREDIENTS

- 1 cup cooked and cooled sweet potato
- 1 banana
- 1/2 cup plain Greek yogurt
- 1/2 cup almond milk
- 1 teaspoon honey
- 1/2 teaspoon ground cinnamon
- 1/4 teaspoon ground nutmeg
- Ice (optional)

DIRECTIONS

1. Add all ingredients to a blender and blend until smooth.
2. If desired, add ice and blend again until desired consistency is reached.
3. Pour into a glass and enjoy!

NUTRITIONAL VALUE:

- Calories: 252
- Protein: 15g
- Fat: 3g
- Carbohydrates: 46g
- Fiber: 7g
- Sugar: 23g

CREAMY PUMPKIN PIE SMOOTHIE

INGREDIENTS

- 1/2 cup pumpkin puree
- 1 banana
- 1/2 cup plain Greek yogurt
- 1/2 cup almond milk
- 1 teaspoon honey
- 1/2 teaspoon ground cinnamon
- 1/4 teaspoon ground ginger
- 1/4 teaspoon ground nutmeg
- Ice (optional)

DIRECTIONS

1. Add all ingredients to a blender and blend until smooth.
2. If desired, add ice and blend again until desired consistency is reached.
3. Pour into a glass and enjoy!

NUTRITIONAL VALUE:

- Calories: 216
- Protein: 14g
- Fat: 3g
- Carbohydrates: 38g
- Fiber: 7g
- Sugar: 20g

SANGRIA SMOOTHIE FOR PARTY

INGREDIENTS

- 1 cup frozen mixed fruit (strawberries, blueberries, raspberries)
- 1/2 cup red wine
- 1/2 cup orange juice
- 1/4 cup pineapple juice
- 1 tablespoon honey
- Ice (optional)
- Fresh fruit and mint leaves for garnish (optional)

DIRECTIONS

1. Add frozen fruit, red wine, orange juice, pineapple juice, and honey to a blender and blend until smooth.
2. If desired, add ice and blend again until desired consistency is reached.
3. Pour into glasses and garnish with fresh fruit and mint leaves, if desired.
4. Enjoy your sangria smoothie!

NUTRITIONAL VALUE:

- Calories: 181
- Protein: 1g
- Fat: 0g
- Carbohydrates: 34g
- Fiber: 3g
- Sugar: 28g

MARGARITA SMOOTHIE FOR PARTY

INGREDIENTS

- 1 cup frozen mango
- 1/2 cup tequila
- 1/2 cup lime juice
- 1/4 cup orange juice
- 1 tablespoon honey
- Salt for rimming glass (optional)
- Lime wedges for garnish (optional)

DIRECTIONS

1. Add frozen mango, tequila, lime juice, orange juice, and honey to a blender and blend until smooth.
2. If desired, rim glasses with salt.
3. Pour smoothie into glasses and garnish with lime wedges, if desired.
4. Enjoy your margarita smoothie!

NUTRITIONAL VALUE:

- Calories: 249
- Protein: 1g
- Fat: 0g
- Carbohydrates: 38g
- Fiber: 2g
- Sugar: 31g

CHAPTER 3.

WINTER SMOOTHIES

APPLE AND CINNAMON WARM WINTER SMOOTHIE

Ingredients

- 2 medium-sized apples, cored and diced
- 1 cup unsweetened almond milk
- 1 teaspoon ground cinnamon
- 1 tablespoon honey
- 1/2 teaspoon vanilla extract
- 1/2 cup boiling water

Directions

1. In a blender, combine the diced apples, almond milk, honey, cinnamon, and vanilla extract.
2. Blend on high speed until smooth and creamy.
3. Pour the mixture into a large mug or bowl.
4. In a small saucepan, bring the water to a boil.
5. Pour the boiling water over the apple mixture and stir until well combined.
6. Serve immediately and enjoy the warm and comforting flavors of the apple and cinnamon smoothie.

Nutritional value

- Calories: 175
- Fat: 2g
- Carbohydrates: 42g
- Protein: 2g
- Fiber: 7g

APPLE AND GINGER WARM WINTER SMOOTHIE

Ingredients

- 2 medium-sized apples, cored and diced
- 1 cup unsweetened almond milk
- 1 tablespoon grated ginger
- 1 tablespoon honey
- 1/2 teaspoon vanilla extract
- 1/2 cup boiling water

Directions

1. In a blender, combine the diced apples, almond milk, ginger, honey, and vanilla extract.
2. Blend on high speed until smooth and creamy.
3. Pour the mixture into a large mug or bowl.
4. In a small saucepan, bring the water to a boil.
5. Pour the boiling water over the apple mixture and stir until well combined.
6. Serve immediately and enjoy the warm and invigorating flavors of the apple and ginger smoothie.

Nutritional value

- Calories: 165
- Fat: 2g
- Carbohydrates: 39g
- Protein: 2g
- Fiber: 7g

PUMPKIN AND SPICE WARM WINTER SMOOTHIE

INGREDIENTS

- 1 cup canned pumpkin puree
- 1 cup unsweetened almond milk
- 1 teaspoon pumpkin pie spice
- 1 tablespoon honey
- 1/2 teaspoon vanilla extract
- 1/2 cup boiling water

DIRECTIONS

1. In a blender, combine the pumpkin puree, almond milk, pumpkin pie spice, honey, and vanilla extract.
2. Blend on high speed until smooth and creamy.
3. Pour the mixture into a large mug or bowl.
4. In a small saucepan, bring the water to a boil.
5. Pour the boiling water over the pumpkin mixture and stir until well combined.
6. Serve immediately and enjoy the warm and cozy flavors of the pumpkin and spice smoothie.

NUTRITIONAL VALUE

- Calories: 120
- Fat: 3g
- Carbohydrates: 23g
- Protein: 2g
- Fiber: 7g

BANANA AND NUTMEG WARM WINTER SMOOTHIE

INGREDIENTS

- 2 medium-sized ripe bananas
- 1 cup unsweetened almond milk
- 1 teaspoon ground nutmeg
- 1 tablespoon honey
- 1/2 teaspoon vanilla extract
- 1/2 cup boiling water

DIRECTIONS

1. In a blender, combine the bananas, almond milk, honey, nutmeg, and vanilla extract.
2. Blend on high speed until smooth and creamy.
3. Pour the mixture into a large mug or bowl.
4. In a small saucepan, bring the water to a boil.
5. Pour the boiling water over the banana mixture and stir until well combined.
6. Serve immediately and enjoy the warm and comforting flavors of the banana and nutmeg smoothie.

NUTRITIONAL VALUE

- Calories: 195
- Fat: 2g
- Carbohydrates: 47g
- Protein: 2g
- Fiber: 5g

CHAPTER 4.

SMOOTHIES BY AGE

KID-FRIENDLY BERRY SMOOTHIE

INGREDIENTS

- 1 cup frozen mixed berries
- 1 ripe banana
- 1 cup unsweetened vanilla almond milk
- 1/4 cup plain Greek yogurt
- 1 teaspoon honey (optional)

DIRECTIONS

1. In a blender, add the frozen mixed berries, banana, almond milk, and Greek yogurt.
2. Blend until smooth and creamy.
3. Taste and add honey if desired for sweetness.
4. Pour into two cups and serve immediately for a healthy and delicious snack.

NUTRITIONAL VALUE

- Calories: 120
- Fat: 2g
- Carbohydrates: 23g
- Protein: 5g
- Fiber: 4g

CHOCOLATE PEANUT BUTTER SMOOTHIE FOR KIDS

INGREDIENTS

- 1 ripe banana
- 1 cup unsweetened vanilla almond milk
- 1 tablespoon natural peanut butter
- 1 tablespoon unsweetened cocoa powder
- 1 teaspoon honey (optional)

DIRECTIONS

1. In a blender, add the ripe banana, almond milk, peanut butter, and cocoa powder.
2. Blend until smooth and creamy.
3. Taste and add honey if desired for sweetness.
4. Pour into two cups and serve immediately for a delicious and nutritious treat.

NUTRITIONAL VALUE

- Calories: 190
- Fat: 8g
- Carbohydrates: 26g
- Protein: 7g
- Fiber: 5g

SENIOR'S IMMUNITY-BOOSTING SMOOTHIE

Ingredients

- 1 medium orange, peeled and segmented
- 1/2 cup frozen pineapple chunks
- 1/2 inch piece of fresh ginger, peeled and grated
- 1/2 cup unsweetened coconut water
- 1/2 cup plain Greek yogurt

Directions

1. In a blender, add the orange segments, frozen pineapple chunks, grated ginger, coconut water, and Greek yogurt.
2. Blend until smooth and creamy.
3. Pour into two cups and serve immediately for a delicious and healthy drink that may boost the immune system.

Nutritional value

- Calories: 95
- Fat: 1g
- Carbohydrates: 17g
- Protein: 6g
- Fiber: 2g

SENIOR'S ANTI-INFLAMMATORY SMOOTHIE

Ingredients

- 1 cup frozen mixed berries
- 1/2 cup unsweetened almond milk
- 1/2 cup plain Greek yogurt
- 1/4 teaspoon ground turmeric
- 1/4 teaspoon ground ginger

Directions

1. In a blender, add the frozen mixed berries, almond milk, Greek yogurt, ground turmeric, and ground ginger.
2. Blend until smooth and creamy.
3. Pour into two cups and serve immediately for a delicious and anti-inflammatory drink that may help reduce joint pain and inflammation.

Nutritional value

- Calories: 80
- Fat: 2g
- Carbohydrates: 11g
- Protein: 7g
- Fiber: 3g

CHAPTER 5.

HEALTH AND WELLNESS SMOOTHIES

GREEN GUT PURIFICATION SMOOTHIE

INGREDIENTS

- 1 cup kale leaves, chopped
- 1/2 avocado, peeled and pitted
- 1/2 cup frozen pineapple chunks
- 1/2 cup frozen mango chunks
- 1/2 inch piece of ginger, peeled
- 1 cup coconut water
- 1 teaspoon honey (optional)

DIRECTIONS

1. Add all ingredients to a blender and blend until smooth and creamy.
2. If the smoothie is too thick, add more coconut water until you reach the desired consistency.
3. Taste and adjust sweetness with honey, if desired.
4. Pour into a glass and enjoy immediately.

NUTRITIONAL VALUE (1 SMOOTHIE)

- Calories: 296
- Fat: 14g
- Carbohydrates: 43g
- Fiber: 10g
- Protein: 6g

BERRY GUT PURIFICATION SMOOTHIE

INGREDIENTS

- 1 cup mixed berries (blueberries, raspberries, blackberries)
- 1 banana, peeled
- 1 cup spinach leaves
- 1/2 cup almond milk
- 1/2 cup plain Greek yogurt
- 1 tablespoon chia seeds
- 1 teaspoon honey (optional)

DIRECTIONS

1. Add all ingredients to a blender and blend until smooth and creamy.
2. If the smoothie is too thick, add more almond milk until you reach the desired consistency.
3. Taste and adjust sweetness with honey, if desired.
4. Pour into a glass and enjoy immediately.

NUTRITIONAL VALUE (1 SMOOTHIE)

- Calories: 293
- Fat: 9g
- Carbohydrates: 44g
- Fiber: 13g
- Protein: 14g

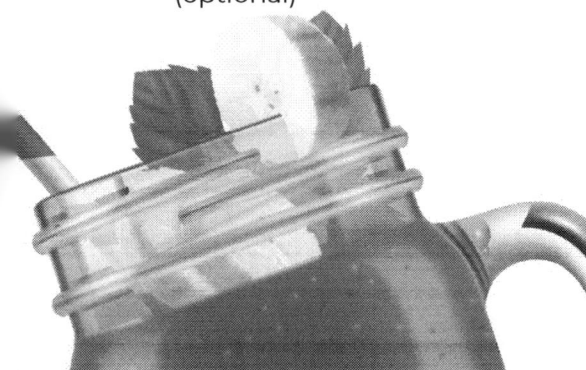

BERRY BANANA SMOOTHIE FOR BONE HEALTH

Ingredients

- 1 banana, peeled
- 1 cup mixed berries (strawberries, raspberries, blueberries)
- 1/2 cup low-fat vanilla Greek yogurt
- 1/2 cup unsweetened almond milk
- 1 tablespoon chia seeds
- 1 teaspoon honey (optional)

Directions

1. Combine all ingredients in a blender.
2. Blend until smooth and creamy.
3. Taste and adjust sweetness with honey, if desired.
4. Pour into a glass and enjoy immediately.

Nutritional value (1 smoothie)

- Calories: 258
- Fat: 6g
- Carbohydrates: 44g
- Fiber: 9g
- Protein: 11g

GREEN SMOOTHIE FOR BONE HEALTH

Ingredients

- 1 cup kale leaves, chopped
- 1 green apple, cored and chopped
- 1/2 avocado, peeled and pitted
- 1/2 cup unsweetened almond milk
- 1/2 cup low-fat vanilla Greek yogurt
- 1/2 inch piece of ginger, peeled
- 1 tablespoon honey (optional)

Directions

1. Combine all ingredients in a blender.
2. Blend until smooth and creamy.
3. Taste and adjust sweetness with honey, if desired.
4. Pour into a glass and enjoy immediately.

Nutritional value (1 smoothie)

- Calories: 258
- Fat: 6g
- Carbohydrates: 44g
- Fiber: 9g
- Protein: 11g

BLUEBERRY BANANA SLIMMING SMOOTHIE

INGREDIENTS

- 1 ripe banana, peeled and sliced
- 1 cup frozen blueberries
- 1/2 cup plain Greek yogurt
- 1/2 cup unsweetened almond milk
- 1 teaspoon honey
- 1/2 teaspoon vanilla extract
- 1 handful baby spinach leaves
- Ice cubes (optional)

DIRECTIONS

1. Combine all ingredients in a blender and blend until smooth.
2. Add ice cubes if desired to thicken the smoothie.
3. Pour into a glass and serve immediately.

NUTRITIONAL VALUE

- Calories: 202
- Protein: 9g
- Fat: 2g
- Carbohydrates: 42g
- Fiber: 7g
- Sugar: 24g
- Sodium: 87mg

GREEN APPLE AND KALE SLIMMING SMOOTHIE

INGREDIENTS

- 1 green apple, cored and chopped
- 1 cup chopped kale leaves
- 1/2 cup chopped celery
- 1/2 cup unsweetened almond milk
- 1/2 cup plain Greek yogurt
- 1 tablespoon chia seeds
- 1 tablespoon honey
- 1/2 teaspoon cinnamon
- Ice cubes (optional)

DIRECTIONS

1. Add all ingredients to a blender and blend until smooth.
2. Add ice cubes if desired to thicken the smoothie.
3. Pour into a glass and serve immediately.

NUTRITIONAL VALUE

- Calories: 206
- Protein: 11g
- Fat: 4g
- Carbohydrates: 36g
- Fiber: 9g
- Sugar: 23g
- Sodium: 116mg

GREEN DETOX SMOOTHIE

INGREDIENTS

- 1 cup chopped kale
- 1 cup spinach leaves
- 1/2 medium-sized cucumber, chopped
- 1/2 ripe avocado
- 1 medium-sized banana
- 1/2 lemon, juiced
- 1 cup unsweetened almond milk
- 1 tablespoon chia seeds

DIRECTIONS

1. Add all ingredients to a blender and blend until smooth.
2. If the mixture is too thick, add more almond milk to reach desired consistency.
3. Pour into a glass and serve immediately.

NUTRITIONAL VALUE

- Calories: 325
- Protein: 10g
- Fat: 19g
- Carbohydrates: 37g
- Fiber: 16g
- Sugar: 13g
- Sodium: 137mg

PINEAPPLE TURMERIC DETOX SMOOTHIE

INGREDIENTS

- 1 cup fresh pineapple chunks
- 1 banana
- 1/2 cup plain Greek yogurt
- 1/2 cup unsweetened almond milk
- 1/2 teaspoon ground turmeric
- 1/2 teaspoon ground ginger
- 1 teaspoon honey
- Ice cubes (optional)

DIRECTIONS

1. Add all ingredients to a blender and blend until smooth.
2. Add ice cubes if desired to thicken the smoothie.
3. Pour into a glass and serve immediately.

NUTRITIONAL VALUE

- Calories: 231
- Protein: 12g
- Fat: 2g
- Carbohydrates: 44g
- Fiber: 4g
- Sugar: 29g
- Sodium: 91mg

BERRY AND OAT SMOOTHIE FOR BLOOD SUGAR REGULATION

INGREDIENTS

- 1/2 cup frozen mixed berries
- 1/2 ripe banana
- 1/2 cup cooked steel-cut oats, cooled
- 1/2 cup unsweetened almond milk
- 1/2 teaspoon vanilla extract
- 1 teaspoon honey
- 1 tablespoon chia seeds

DIRECTIONS

1. Combine all ingredients in a blender and blend until smooth.
2. If the mixture is too thick, add more almond milk to reach desired consistency.
3. Pour into a glass and serve immediately.

NUTRITIONAL VALUE

- Calories: 292
- Protein: 10g
- Fat: 8g
- Carbohydrates: 49g
- Fiber: 12g
- Sugar: 14g
- Sodium: 81mg

GREEN SMOOTHIE FOR BLOOD SUGAR REGULATION

INGREDIENTS

- 1 cup baby spinach leaves
- 1/2 medium-sized cucumber, chopped
- 1/2 medium-sized green apple, chopped
- 1/2 lemon, juiced
- 1/2 teaspoon grated ginger
- 1/2 cup unsweetened almond milk
- 1/2 teaspoon cinnamon
- Ice cubes (optional)

DIRECTIONS

1. Combine all ingredients in a blender and blend until smooth.
2. If the mixture is too thick, add more almond milk to reach desired consistency.
3. Add ice cubes if desired to thicken the smoothie.
4. Pour into a glass and serve immediately.

NUTRITIONAL VALUE

- Calories: 121
- Protein: 3g
- Fat: 2g
- Carbohydrates: 26g
- Fiber: 6g
- Sugar: 16g
- Sodium: 85mg

BEET AND BERRY SMOOTHIE FOR CIRCULATION

Ingredients

- 1 small beet, peeled and chopped
- 1 cup frozen mixed berries
- 1/2 cup unsweetened almond milk
- 1/2 cup plain Greek yogurt
- 1/2 teaspoon grated ginger
- 1 teaspoon honey
- Ice cubes (optional)

Directions

1. Add all ingredients to a blender and blend until smooth.
2. If the mixture is too thick, add more almond milk to reach desired consistency.
3. Add ice cubes if desired to thicken the smoothie.
4. Pour into a glass and serve immediately.

Nutritional value

- Calories: 208
- Protein: 11g
- Fat: 2g
- Carbohydrates: 37g
- Fiber: 8g
- Sugar: 24g
- Sodium: 148mg

PINEAPPLE GINGER SMOOTHIE FOR CIRCULATION

Ingredients

- 1 cup fresh pineapple chunks
- 1 banana
- 1/2 inch piece of fresh ginger, peeled and chopped
- 1/2 cup unsweetened almond milk
- 1/2 teaspoon ground turmeric
- 1 teaspoon honey
- Ice cubes (optional)

Directions

1. Add all ingredients to a blender and blend until smooth.
2. If the mixture is too thick, add more almond milk to reach desired consistency.
3. Add ice cubes if desired to thicken the smoothie.
4. Pour into a glass and serve immediately.

Nutritional value

- Calories: 207
- Protein: 4g
- Fat: 2g
- Carbohydrates: 50g
- Fiber: 6g
- Sugar: 30g
- Sodium: 93mg

BLUEBERRY AND AVOCADO SMOOTHIE FOR HORMONE FUNCTION REGULATION

Ingredients

- 1/2 ripe avocado
- 1/2 cup frozen blueberries
- 1/2 cup unsweetened almond milk
- 1/2 teaspoon cinnamon
- 1 teaspoon honey
- 1/2 teaspoon vanilla extract

Directions

1. Add all ingredients to a blender and blend until smooth.
2. If the mixture is too thick, add more almond milk to reach desired consistency.
3. Pour into a glass and serve immediately.

Nutritional value

- Calories: 220
- Protein: 3g
- Fat: 15g
- Carbohydrates: 23g
- Fiber: 8g
- Sugar: 10g
- Sodium: 84mg

BERRY AND FLAXSEED SMOOTHIE FOR HORMONE FUNCTION REGULATION

Ingredients

- 1/2 cup frozen mixed berries
- 1/2 ripe banana
- 1/2 cup plain Greek yogurt
- 1/2 cup unsweetened almond milk
- 1 tablespoon ground flaxseed
- 1/2 teaspoon cinnamon
- 1 teaspoon honey

Directions

1. Add all ingredients to a blender and blend until smooth.
2. If the mixture is too thick, add more almond milk to reach desired consistency.
3. Pour into a glass and serve immediately.

Nutritional value

- Calories: 228
- Protein: 13g
- Fat: 7g
- Carbohydrates: 32g
- Fiber: 7g
- Sugar: 19g
- Sodium: 97mg

COCONUT WATER AND PINEAPPLE SMOOTHIE

INGREDIENTS

- 1 cup coconut water
- 1 cup frozen pineapple chunks
- 1 banana
- 1/2 cup Greek yogurt
- 1 tablespoon honey

DIRECTIONS

1. Combine all ingredients in a blender and blend until smooth.
2. Pour into a glass and enjoy!

NUTRITIONAL VALUE:

- Calories: 295
- Protein: 11g
- Fat: 2g
- Carbohydrates: 63g
- Fiber: 5g
- Sugar: 43g
- Sodium: 201mg
- Potassium: 986mg
- Vitamin C: 111% RDI

WATERMELON AND MINT SMOOTHIE

INGREDIENTS

- 2 cups cubed watermelon
- 1/2 cup coconut water
- 1/4 cup fresh mint leaves
- 1 tablespoon lime juice
- 1 teaspoon honey
- 1/2 cup ice

DIRECTIONS

1. Combine all ingredients in a blender and blend until smooth.
2. Pour into a glass and enjoy!

NUTRITIONAL VALUE:

- Calories: 107
- Protein: 2g
- Fat: 0g
- Carbohydrates: 27g
- Fiber: 1g
- Sugar: 21g
- Sodium: 152mg
- Potassium: 478mg
- Vitamin C: 31% RDI

BERRY BLAST SMOOTHIE

INGREDIENTS

- 1 cup mixed berries (strawberries, blueberries, raspberries)
- 1 banana
- 1 cup unsweetened almond milk
- 1/2 cup Greek yogurt
- 1 tablespoon chia seeds
- 1 teaspoon honey
- 1/2 cup ice

DIRECTIONS

1. Combine all ingredients in a blender and blend until smooth.
2. Pour into a glass and enjoy!

NUTRITIONAL VALUE:

- Calories: 326
- Protein: 16g
- Fat: 10g
- Carbohydrates: 50g
- Fiber: 14g
- Sugar: 26g
- Sodium: 174mg
- Potassium: 703mg
- Vitamin C: 68% RDI

GREEN GOODNESS SMOOTHIE

INGREDIENTS

- 2 cups spinach
- 1 banana
- 1 cup unsweetened almond milk
- 1/4 cup fresh mint leaves
- 1/4 avocado
- 1/2 lemon, juiced
- 1/2 cup ice

DIRECTIONS

1. Combine all ingredients in a blender and blend until smooth.
2. Pour into a glass and enjoy!

NUTRITIONAL VALUE:

- Calories: 228
- Protein: 7g
- Fat: 12g
- Carbohydrates: 29g
- Fiber: 9g
- Sugar: 12g
- Sodium: 255mg
- Potassium: 1037mg
- Vitamin C: 71% RDI

BERRY AND FLAXSEED SMOOTHIE

INGREDIENTS

- 1 cup mixed berries (strawberries, blueberries, raspberries)
- 1/2 cup Greek yogurt
- 1/4 cup flaxseeds
- 1/2 banana
- 1 cup unsweetened almond milk
- 1 tablespoon honey
- 1/2 cup ice

DIRECTIONS

1. Combine all ingredients in a blender and blend until smooth.
2. Pour into a glass and enjoy!

NUTRITIONAL VALUE:

- Calories: 334
- Protein: 19g
- Fat: 17g
- Carbohydrates: 34g
- Fiber: 13g
- Sugar: 17g
- Sodium: 191mg
- Potassium: 634mg
- Vitamin C: 67% RDI

GREEN TEA AND SOY SMOOTHIE

INGREDIENTS

- 1 cup brewed green tea, cooled
- 1/2 cup unsweetened soy milk
- 1 banana
- 1/2 cup frozen pineapple chunks
- 1 tablespoon honey
- 1/2 teaspoon grated ginger

DIRECTIONS

1. Combine all ingredients in a blender and blend until smooth.
2. Pour into a glass and enjoy!

NUTRITIONAL VALUE:

- Calories: 203
- Protein: 5g
- Fat: 2g
- Carbohydrates: 48g
- Fiber: 5g
- Sugar: 32g
- Sodium: 46mg
- Potassium: 611mg
- Vitamin C: 45% RDI

PREGNANCY POWER SMOOTHIE

Ingredients

- 1 banana
- 1/2 cup frozen strawberries
- 1/2 cup frozen blueberries
- 1/2 cup Greek yogurt
- 1/2 cup spinach
- 1/2 cup unsweetened almond milk
- 1 tablespoon chia seeds

Directions

1. Combine all ingredients in a blender and blend until smooth.
2. Pour into a glass and enjoy!

Nutritional value:

- Calories: 280
- Protein: 17g
- Fat: 7g
- Carbohydrates: 42g
- Fiber: 11g
- Sugar: 23g
- Sodium: 110mg
- Potassium: 804mg
- Vitamin C: 64% RDI

MANGO AND AVOCADO SMOOTHIE

Ingredients

- 1 ripe mango, peeled and cubed
- 1/2 avocado, pitted and peeled
- 1/2 cup Greek yogurt
- 1/2 cup unsweetened coconut milk
- 1 tablespoon honey
- 1/2 lime, juiced
- 1/2 cup ice

Directions

1. Combine all ingredients in a blender and blend until smooth.
2. Pour into a glass and enjoy!

Nutritional value:

- Calories: 344
- Protein: 13g
- Fat: 16g
- Carbohydrates: 43g
- Fiber: 9g
- Sugar: 31g
- Sodium: 92mg
- Potassium: 821mg
- Vitamin C: 94% RDI

PEANUT BUTTER AND BANANA SOY MILK SMOOTHIE

INGREDIENTS

- 1 banana
- 1/4 cup natural peanut butter
- 1 cup unsweetened soy milk
- 1/2 cup ice
- 1 tablespoon honey (optional)

DIRECTIONS

1. Combine all ingredients in a blender and blend until smooth.
2. Pour into a glass and enjoy!

NUTRITIONAL VALUE:

- Calories: 438
- Protein: 19g
- Fat: 23g
- Carbohydrates: 42g
- Fiber: 6g
- Sugar: 20g
- Sodium: 219mg
- Potassium: 708mg
- Vitamin C: 10% RDI

BLUEBERRY AND VANILLA SOY MILK SMOOTHIE

INGREDIENTS

- 1 cup frozen blueberries
- 1/2 cup unsweetened vanilla soy milk
- 1/2 cup plain Greek yogurt
- 1 tablespoon honey
- 1/2 teaspoon vanilla extract
- 1/2 cup ice

DIRECTIONS

1. Combine all ingredients in a blender and blend until smooth.
2. Pour into a glass and enjoy!

NUTRITIONAL VALUE:

- Calories: 200
- Protein: 12g
- Fat: 3g
- Carbohydrates: 33g
- Fiber: 3g
- Sugar: 25g
- Sodium: 58mg
- Potassium: 343mg
- Vitamin C: 14% RDI

CHOCOLATE BANANA PROTEIN SMOOTHIE

INGREDIENTS

- 1 banana
- 1 scoop chocolate whey protein powder
- 1 cup unsweetened almond milk
- 1 tablespoon natural peanut butter
- 1/2 teaspoon vanilla extract
- 1/2 cup ice

DIRECTIONS

1. Combine all ingredients in a blender and blend until smooth.
2. Pour into a glass and enjoy!

NUTRITIONAL VALUE:

- Calories: 360
- Protein: 34g
- Fat: 13g
- Carbohydrates: 31g
- Fiber: 6g
- Sugar: 16g
- Sodium: 367mg
- Potassium: 647mg

TROPICAL GREEN PROTEIN SMOOTHIE

INGREDIENTS

- 1 cup frozen tropical fruit mix (pineapple, mango, and papaya)
- 1 scoop vanilla whey protein powder
- 1 cup unsweetened coconut milk
- 1/2 cup fresh spinach leaves
- 1 tablespoon chia seeds
- 1/2 cup ice

DIRECTIONS

1. Combine all ingredients in a blender and blend until smooth.
2. Pour into a glass and enjoy!

NUTRITIONAL VALUE:

- Calories: 395
- Protein: 24g
- Fat: 18g
- Carbohydrates: 42g
- Fiber: 10g
- Sugar: 28g
- Sodium: 105mg
- Potassium: 699mg

BERRY ACAI SMOOTHIE BOWL

INGREDIENTS

- 1 frozen banana
- 1/2 cup frozen mixed berries (strawberries, blueberries, raspberries)
- 1 tablespoon acai powder
- 1/2 cup unsweetened almond milk
- 1 teaspoon honey (optional)
- 1 tablespoon chia seeds
- 1/4 cup granola
- 1/4 cup fresh berries (optional)

DIRECTIONS

1. Add the frozen banana, mixed berries, acai powder, almond milk, and honey (if using) to a blender. Blend until smooth.
2. Pour the smoothie into a bowl.
3. Top with chia seeds, granola, and fresh berries (if using).
4. Enjoy!

NUTRITIONAL INFORMATION

- Calories: 346
- Protein: 7g
- Fat: 12g
- Carbohydrates: 54g
- Fiber: 14g
- Sugar: 22g

TROPICAL GREEN SMOOTHIE BOWL

INGREDIENTS

- 1 frozen banana
- 1/2 cup frozen pineapple
- 1/2 cup frozen mango
- 1/2 avocado
- 1 cup spinach
- 1/2 cup unsweetened almond milk
- 1 tablespoon hemp seeds
- 1/4 cup granola
- 1/4 cup sliced banana (optional)

DIRECTIONS

1. Add the frozen banana, pineapple, mango, avocado, spinach, and almond milk to a blender. Blend until smooth.
2. Pour the smoothie into a bowl.
3. Top with hemp seeds, granola, and sliced banana (if using).
4. Enjoy!

NUTRITIONAL INFORMATION

- Calories: 442
- Protein: 10g
- Fat: 21g
- Carbohydrates: 60g
- Fiber: 15g
- Sugar: 30g

CHOCOLATE AVOCADO SMOOTHIE

INGREDIENTS

- 1/2 avocado
- 1 tablespoon unsweetened cocoa powder
- 1 tablespoon honey
- 1/2 cup unsweetened almond milk
- 1/2 cup ice cubes
- 1/2 teaspoon vanilla extract

DIRECTIONS

1. Add the avocado, cocoa powder, honey, almond milk, ice cubes, and vanilla extract to a blender.
2. Blend until smooth and creamy.
3. Pour into a glass and enjoy!

NUTRITIONAL INFORMATION

- Calories: 192
- Protein: 2g
- Fat: 11g
- Carbohydrates: 25g
- Fiber: 6g
- Sugar: 17g

CITRUS SUNRISE SMOOTHIE

INGREDIENTS

- 1 orange, peeled and segmented
- 1/2 grapefruit, peeled and segmented
- 1 banana
- 1/2 cup unsweetened almond milk
- 1 teaspoon honey (optional)
- 1 cup ice cubes

DIRECTIONS

1. Add the orange, grapefruit, banana, almond milk, honey (if using), and ice cubes to a blender.
2. Blend until smooth and creamy.
3. Pour into a glass and enjoy!

NUTRITIONAL INFORMATION

- Calories: 205
- Protein: 3g
- Fat: 1g
- Carbohydrates: 51g
- Fiber: 7g
- Sugar: 32g

GREEN ENERGY SMOOTHIE

Ingredients

- 1 cup spinach
- 1/2 cup kale
- 1/2 avocado
- 1/2 banana
- 1/2 cup unsweetened almond milk
- 1 tablespoon honey (optional)
- 1 tablespoon chia seeds

Directions

1. Add the spinach, kale, avocado, banana, almond milk, honey (if using), and chia seeds to a blender.
2. Blend until smooth and creamy.
3. Pour into a glass and enjoy!

Nutritional Information

- Calories: 269
- Protein: 8g
- Fat: 15g
- Carbohydrates: 32g
- Fiber: 14g
- Sugar: 13g

TROPICAL TURMERIC SMOOTHIE

Ingredients

- 1/2 cup frozen pineapple chunks
- 1/2 banana
- 1/2 cup unsweetened coconut milk
- 1/4 cup orange juice
- 1 teaspoon turmeric powder
- 1 teaspoon grated ginger
- 1 cup ice cubes

Directions

1. Add the pineapple chunks, banana, coconut milk, orange juice, turmeric powder, grated ginger, and ice cubes to a blender.
2. Blend until smooth and creamy.
3. Pour into a glass and enjoy!

Nutritional Information

- Calories: 150
- Protein: 1g
- Fat: 4g
- Carbohydrates: 29g
- Fiber: 3g
- Sugar: 19g

GINGER SPICE SMOOTHIE

INGREDIENTS

- 1 orange, peeled and segmented
- 1 banana
- 1/2 cup unsweetened almond milk
- 1/2 inch piece of fresh ginger, peeled and grated
- 1/4 teaspoon ground cinnamon
- 1 cup ice cubes

DIRECTIONS

1. Add the orange, banana, almond milk, grated ginger, cinnamon, and ice cubes to a blender.
2. Blend until smooth and creamy.
3. Pour into a glass and enjoy!

NUTRITIONAL INFORMATION

- Calories: 180
- Protein: 3g
- Fat: 2g
- Carbohydrates: 42g
- Fiber: 7g
- Sugar: 25g

GREEN IMMUNITY BOOST SMOOTHIE

INGREDIENTS

- 1/2 cup kale
- 1/2 cup spinach
- 1/2 avocado
- 1/2 banana
- 1/2 cup unsweetened almond milk
- 1/4 cup Greek yogurt
- 1 teaspoon honey (optional)
- 1 cup ice cubes

DIRECTIONS

1. Add the kale, spinach, avocado, banana, almond milk, Greek yogurt, honey (if using), and ice cubes to a blender.
2. Blend until smooth and creamy.
3. Pour into a glass and enjoy!

NUTRITIONAL INFORMATION

- Calories: 244
- Protein: 9g
- Fat: 14g
- Carbohydrates: 25g
- Fiber: 8g
- Sugar: 10g

BERRY BEAUTY SMOOTHIE

Ingredients

- 1 cup mixed berries (strawberries, raspberries, blueberries)
- 1/2 cup coconut water
- 1/2 cup plain Greek yogurt
- 1/2 banana
- 1 tablespoon honey (optional)
- 1 cup ice cubes

Directions

1. Add the mixed berries, coconut water, Greek yogurt, banana, honey (if using), and ice cubes to a blender.
2. Blend until smooth and creamy.
3. Pour into a glass and enjoy!

Nutritional Information

- Calories: 178
- Protein: 10g
- Fat: 2g
- Carbohydrates: 34g
- Fiber: 6g
- Sugar: 23g

CITRUS GLOW SMOOTHIE

Ingredients

- 1 orange, peeled and segmented
- 1/2 cup chopped carrots
- 1/2 cup unsweetened almond milk
- 1/2 cup plain Greek yogurt
- 1 tablespoon chia seeds
- 1 cup ice cubes

Directions

1. Add the orange, chopped carrots, almond milk, Greek yogurt, chia seeds, and ice cubes to a blender.
2. Blend until smooth and creamy.
3. Pour into a glass and enjoy!

Nutritional Information

- Calories: 209
- Protein: 13g
- Fat: 5g
- Carbohydrates: 33g
- Fiber: 10g
- Sugar: 19g

BLUEBERRY BRAIN BOOST SMOOTHIE

INGREDIENTS

- 1 cup blueberries
- 1 banana
- 1/2 cup plain Greek yogurt
- 1/2 cup unsweetened almond milk
- 1 tablespoon almond butter
- 1 teaspoon honey (optional)
- 1 cup ice cubes

DIRECTIONS

1. Add the blueberries, banana, Greek yogurt, almond milk, almond butter, honey (if using), and ice cubes to a blender.
2. Blend until smooth and creamy.
3. Pour into a glass and enjoy!

NUTRITIONAL INFORMATION

- Calories: 262
- Protein: 13g
- Fat: 10g
- Carbohydrates: 35g
- Fiber: 6g
- Sugar: 20g

GREEN MENTAL CLARITY SMOOTHIE

INGREDIENTS

- 1/2 cup spinach
- 1/2 cup kale
- 1/2 avocado
- 1/2 banana
- 1/2 cup unsweetened almond milk
- 1 tablespoon chia seeds
- 1 teaspoon honey (optional)
- 1 cup ice cubes

DIRECTIONS

1. Add the spinach, kale, avocado, banana, almond milk, chia seeds, honey (if using), and ice cubes to a blender.
2. Blend until smooth and creamy.
3. Pour into a glass and enjoy!

NUTRITIONAL INFORMATION

- Calories: 259
- Protein: 8g
- Fat: 15g
- Carbohydrates: 29g
- Fiber: 12g
- Sugar: 10g

BANANA BRAIN BOOSTER SMOOTHIE

INGREDIENTS

- 1 banana
- 1/2 cup blueberries
- 1/2 cup unsweetened almond milk
- 1/2 cup plain Greek yogurt
- 1 tablespoon honey (optional)
- 1 tablespoon ground flaxseed
- 1 cup ice cubes

DIRECTIONS

1. Add the banana, blueberries, almond milk, Greek yogurt, honey (if using), ground flaxseed, and ice cubes to a blender.
2. Blend until smooth and creamy.
3. Pour into a glass and enjoy!

NUTRITIONAL INFORMATION

- Calories: 228
- Protein: 12g
- Fat: 5g
- Carbohydrates: 38g
- Fiber: 6g
- Sugar: 25g

BRAIN POWER SMOOTHIE

INGREDIENTS

- 1/2 avocado
- 1/2 banana
- 1/2 cup unsweetened almond milk
- 1/2 cup blueberries
- 1 tablespoon honey (optional)
- 1 tablespoon almond butter
- 1 cup ice cubes

DIRECTIONS

1. Add the avocado, banana, almond milk, blueberries, honey (if using), almond butter, and ice cubes to a blender.
2. Blend until smooth and creamy.
3. Pour into a glass and enjoy!

NUTRITIONAL INFORMATION

- Calories: 272
- Protein: 7g
- Fat: 18g
- Carbohydrates: 26g
- Fiber: 8g
- Sugar: 13g

MANGO GINGER BLISS SMOOTHIE

Ingredients

- 1 cup frozen mango
- 1 banana
- 1/2 cup plain Greek yogurt
- 1/2 cup unsweetened almond milk
- 1 tablespoon grated ginger
- 1 tablespoon honey (optional)
- 1 cup ice cubes

Directions

1. Add the frozen mango, banana, Greek yogurt, almond milk, grated ginger, honey (if using), and ice cubes to a blender.
2. Blend until smooth and creamy.
3. Pour into a glass and enjoy!

Nutritional Information

- Calories: 268
- Protein: 14g
- Fat: 4g
- Carbohydrates: 51g
- Fiber: 4g
- Sugar: 37g

LAVENDER RELAXATION SMOOTHIE

Ingredients

- 1/2 banana
- 1/2 cup unsweetened almond milk
- 1/2 cup blueberries
- 1/2 cup plain Greek yogurt
- 1 teaspoon dried lavender buds
- 1 teaspoon honey (optional)
- 1 cup ice cubes

Directions

1. Add the banana, almond milk, blueberries, Greek yogurt, dried lavender buds, honey (if using), and ice cubes to a blender.
2. Blend until smooth and creamy.
3. Pour into a glass and enjoy!

Nutritional Information

- Calories: 193
- Protein: 12g
- Fat: 3g
- Carbohydrates: 32g
- Fiber: 3g
- Sugar: 21g

PEANUT BUTTER BANANA PROTEIN SMOOTHIE

INGREDIENTS

- 1 banana
- 1/2 cup plain Greek yogurt
- 1 tablespoon peanut butter
- 1/2 cup unsweetened almond milk
- 1 scoop vanilla protein powder
- 1 teaspoon honey (optional)
- 1 cup ice cubes

DIRECTIONS

1. Add the banana, Greek yogurt, peanut butter, almond milk, protein powder, honey (if using), and ice cubes to a blender.
2. Blend until smooth and creamy.
3. Pour into a glass and enjoy!

NUTRITIONAL INFORMATION

- Calories: 366
- Protein: 37g
- Fat: 12g
- Carbohydrates: 32g
- Fiber: 4g
- Sugar: 17g

CHOCOLATE BERRY PROTEIN SMOOTHIE

INGREDIENTS

- 1 cup frozen mixed berries
- 1/2 cup plain Greek yogurt
- 1/2 cup unsweetened almond milk
- 1 scoop chocolate protein powder
- 1 teaspoon honey (optional)
- 1 cup ice cubes

DIRECTIONS

1. Add the frozen mixed berries, Greek yogurt, almond milk, chocolate protein powder, honey (if using), and ice cubes to a blender.
2. Blend until smooth and creamy.
3. Pour into a glass and enjoy!

NUTRITIONAL INFORMATION

- Calories: 262
- Protein: 29g
- Fat: 4g
- Carbohydrates: 31g
- Fiber: 6g
- Sugar: 17g

CHAPTER 6.

FOOD INTOLERANCE AND ALLERGY SMOOTHIES

BANANA OAT SMOOTHIE

INGREDIENTS

- 1 medium-sized ripe banana
- 1 cup of unsweetened oat milk
- 1/2 cup of plain Greek yogurt
- 1 tablespoon of honey
- 1/4 teaspoon of ground cinnamon
- 1 cup of ice

DIRECTIONS

1. Peel the banana and chop it into small pieces.
2. Add the chopped banana, oat milk, Greek yogurt, honey, and ground cinnamon to a blender.
3. Blend the ingredients on high speed until the mixture is smooth.
4. Add the ice to the blender and blend again until the ice is completely crushed.
5. Pour the smoothie into a glass and serve immediately.

NUTRITIONAL INFORMATION

- Calories: 265
- Protein: 12g
- Fat: 4g
- Carbohydrates: 50g
- Fiber: 4g
- Sugar: 28g
- Sodium: 120mg

BERRY SPINACH SMOOTHIE

INGREDIENTS

- 1 cup of fresh spinach
- 1 cup of frozen mixed berries
- 1 cup of unsweetened coconut milk
- 1/2 cup of plain Greek yogurt
- 1 tablespoon of honey
- 1/2 teaspoon of vanilla extract

DIRECTIONS

1. Add the spinach, frozen berries, coconut milk, Greek yogurt, honey, and vanilla extract to a blender.
2. Blend the ingredients on high speed until the mixture is smooth.
3. If the smoothie is too thick, add more coconut milk until it reaches your desired consistency.
4. Pour the smoothie into a glass and serve immediately.

NUTRITIONAL INFORMATION

- Calories: 190
- Protein: 8g
- Fat: 7g
- Carbohydrates: 26g
- Fiber: 6g
- Sugar: 17g
- Sodium: 90mg

MANGO COCONUT SMOOTHIE

Ingredients

- 1 large ripe mango, peeled and chopped
- 1 cup unsweetened coconut milk
- 1/2 cup plain Greek yogurt
- 1 tablespoon honey
- 1/2 teaspoon vanilla extract
- 1 cup ice cubes

Directions

1. Add the chopped mango, coconut milk, Greek yogurt, honey, and vanilla extract to a blender.
2. Blend the ingredients on high speed until the mixture is smooth.
3. Add the ice cubes to the blender and blend again until the ice is completely crushed.
4. Pour the smoothie into a glass and serve immediately.

Nutritional Information

- Calories: 260
- Protein: 9g
- Fat: 11g
- Carbohydrates: 36g
- Fiber: 3g
- Sugar: 32g
- Sodium: 85mg

BERRY BANANA SMOOTHIE

Ingredients

- 1 large ripe banana, peeled and sliced
- 1 cup frozen mixed berries
- 1 cup unsweetened almond milk
- 1/2 cup plain Greek yogurt
- 1 tablespoon honey
- 1 cup ice cubes

Directions

1. Add the sliced banana, mixed berries, almond milk, honey and Greek yogurt to a blender.
2. Blend the ingredients on high speed until the mixture is smooth.
3. Add the ice cubes to the blender and blend again until the ice is completely crushed.
4. Pour the smoothie into a glass and serve immediately.

Nutritional Information

- Calories: 240
- Protein: 9g
- Fat: 4g
- Carbohydrates: 44g
- Fiber: 7g
- Sugar: 30g
- Sodium: 180mg

PEACH GINGER SMOOTHIE

INGREDIENTS

- 2 ripe peaches, peeled and sliced
- 1/2 teaspoon grated fresh ginger
- 1 cup unsweetened coconut milk
- 1/2 cup plain Greek yogurt
- 1 tablespoon honey
- 1 cup ice cubes

DIRECTIONS

1. Add the sliced peaches, grated ginger, coconut milk, Greek yogurt, and honey to a blender.
2. Blend the ingredients on high speed until the mixture is smooth.
3. Add the ice cubes to the blender and blend again until the ice is completely crushed.
4. Pour the smoothie into a glass and serve immediately.

NUTRITIONAL INFORMATION

- Calories: 220
- Protein: 9g
- Fat: 7g
- Carbohydrates: 35g
- Fiber: 3g
- Sugar: 27g
- Sodium: 75mg

BLUEBERRY BANANA SMOOTHIE

INGREDIENTS

- 1 large ripe banana, peeled and sliced
- 1 cup frozen blueberries
- 1 cup unsweetened vanilla almond milk
- 1/2 cup plain Greek yogurt
- 1 tablespoon honey
- 1 cup ice cubes

DIRECTIONS

1. Add the sliced banana, blueberries, almond milk, Greek yogurt, and honey to a blender.
2. Blend the ingredients on high speed until the mixture is smooth.
3. Add the ice cubes to the blender and blend again until the ice is completely crushed.
4. Pour the smoothie into a glass and serve immediately.

NUTRITIONAL INFORMATION

- Calories: 220
- Protein: 9g
- Fat: 4g
- Carbohydrates: 40g
- Fiber: 7g
- Sugar: 27g
- Sodium: 180mg

STRAWBERRY COCONUT SMOOTHIE

INGREDIENTS

- 1 cup frozen strawberries
- 1/2 cup unsweetened coconut milk
- 1/2 cup unsweetened almond milk
- 1 tablespoon honey
- 1/4 teaspoon vanilla extract
- 1/2 avocado, pitted and peeled

DIRECTIONS

1. Add the frozen strawberries, coconut milk, almond milk, honey, vanilla extract, and avocado to a blender.
2. Blend the ingredients on high speed until the mixture is smooth.
3. If the smoothie is too thick, add more almond milk until the desired consistency is reached.
4. Pour the smoothie into a glass and serve immediately.

NUTRITIONAL INFORMATION

- Calories: 190
- Protein: 2g
- Fat: 15g
- Carbohydrates: 14g
- Fiber: 6g
- Sugar: 7g
- Sodium: 40mg

BERRY NUT SMOOTHIE

INGREDIENTS

- 1 cup frozen mixed berries
- 1/2 cup unsweetened almond milk
- 1/2 cup unsweetened coconut milk
- 2 tablespoons almond butter
- 1 tablespoon honey
- 1/4 teaspoon vanilla extract

DIRECTIONS

1. Add the frozen mixed berries, almond milk, coconut milk, almond butter, honey, and vanilla extract to a blender.
2. Blend the ingredients on high speed until the mixture is smooth.
3. If the smoothie is too thick, add more almond milk until the desired consistency is reached.
4. Pour the smoothie into a glass and serve immediately.

NUTRITIONAL INFORMATION

- Calories: 240
- Protein: 5g
- Fat: 20g
- Carbohydrates: 16g
- Fiber: 6g
- Sugar: 8g
- Sodium: 90mg

TROPICAL GREEN SMOOTHIE

Ingredients

- 1 cup chopped kale leaves
- 1/2 cup frozen mango chunks
- 1/2 cup frozen pineapple chunks
- 1/2 banana, peeled and sliced
- 1/2 cup unsweetened coconut water
- 1 tablespoon chia seeds

Directions

1. Add the chopped kale leaves, frozen mango chunks, frozen pineapple chunks, sliced banana, coconut water, and chia seeds to a blender.
2. Blend the ingredients on high speed until the mixture is smooth.
3. If the smoothie is too thick, add more coconut water until the desired consistency is reached.
4. Pour the smoothie into a glass and serve immediately.

Nutritional Information

- Calories: 220
- Protein: 6g
- Fat: 4g
- Carbohydrates: 44g
- Fiber: 11g
- Sugar: 25g
- Sodium: 90mg

THANK YOU FOR READING MY BOOK!
I HOPE YOU FOUND IT USEFUL AND THAT THE RECIPES WERE TASTY.

IF YOU ENJOYED THIS COOKBOOK,
PLEASE WRITE A REVIEW.

INDEX OF RECIPES IN ALPHABETICAL ORDER

APPLE AND CINNAMON WARM WINTER SMOOTHIE	48
APPLE AND GINGER WARM WINTER SMOOTHIE	48
APPLE CINNAMON SMOOTHIE	29
AVOCADO LIME SMOOTHIE	34
BANANA AND NUTMEG WARM WINTER SMOOTHIE	49
BANANA BRAIN BOOSTER SMOOTHIE	73
BANANA NUTELLA SMOOTHIE	32
BANANA OAT SMOOTHIE	77
BEET AND BERRY SMOOTHIE FOR CIRCULATION	59
BEETROOT APPLE SMOOTHIE	37
BERRY ACAI SMOOTHIE BOWL	67
BERRY AND FLAXSEED SMOOTHIE	63
BERRY AND FLAXSEED SMOOTHIE FOR HORMONE FUNCTION REGULATION	60
BERRY AND OAT SMOOTHIE FOR BLOOD SUGAR REGULATION	58
BERRY BANANA SMOOTHIE	78
BERRY BANANA SMOOTHIE FOR BONE HEALTH	55
BERRY BEAUTY SMOOTHIE	71
BERRY BLAST SMOOTHIE	62
BERRY GUT PURIFICATION SMOOTHIE	54
BERRY NUT SMOOTHIE	80
BERRY SPINACH SMOOTHIE	77
BLUEBERRY AND AVOCADO SMOOTHIE FOR HORMONE FUNCTION REGULATION	60
BLUEBERRY AND VANILLA SOY MILK SMOOTHIE	65
BLUEBERRY BANANA SLIMMING SMOOTHIE	56
BLUEBERRY BANANA SMOOTHIE	79
BLUEBERRY BRAIN BOOST SMOOTHIE	72
BLUEBERRY LAVENDER CALM SMOOTHIE	43
BLUEBERRY OATMEAL SMOOTHIE	27
BRAIN POWER SMOOTHIE	73
BROCCOLI CHEDDAR SMOOTHIE	36
CAPRESE SALAD SMOOTHIE	39
CARROT CAKE SMOOTHIE	31
CHICKEN CAESAR SMOOTHIE	35
CHOCOLATE AVOCADO SMOOTHIE	68
CHOCOLATE BANANA ALMOND SMOOTHIE	28
CHOCOLATE BANANA PROTEIN SMOOTHIE	66
CHOCOLATE BERRY PROTEIN SMOOTHIE	75
CHOCOLATE PEANUT BUTTER CUP SMOOTHIE	31

CHOCOLATE PEANUT BUTTER SMOOTHIE FOR KIDS	51
CITRUS GLOW SMOOTHIE	71
CITRUS SUNRISE SMOOTHIE	68
COCONUT WATER AND PINEAPPLE SMOOTHIE	61
CREAMY PUMPKIN PIE SMOOTHIE	45
CUCUMBER MINT REFRESH SMOOTHIE	42
GINGER PEACH ANTI-INFLAMMATORY SMOOTHIE	44
GINGER SPICE SMOOTHIE	70
GREEK SALAD SMOOTHIE	35
GREEN APPLE AND KALE SLIMMING SMOOTHIE	56
GREEN DETOX SMOOTHIE	57
GREEN ENERGY SMOOTHIE	69
GREEN GOODNESS SMOOTHIE	62
GREEN GUT PURIFICATION SMOOTHIE	54
GREEN IMMUNITY BOOST SMOOTHIE	70
GREEN MENTAL CLARITY SMOOTHIE	72
GREEN SMOOTHIE FOR BLOOD SUGAR REGULATION	58
GREEN SMOOTHIE FOR BONE HEALTH	55
GREEN TEA AND SOY SMOOTHIE	63
HUMMUS VEGGIE SMOOTHIE	39
KID-FRIENDLY BERRY SMOOTHIE	51
LAVENDER RELAXATION SMOOTHIE	74
LEMON TURMERIC DETOX SMOOTHIE	41
MANGO AND AVOCADO SMOOTHIE	64
MANGO COCONUT SMOOTHIE	78
MANGO GINGER BLISS SMOOTHIE	74
MANGO GINGER DIGESTIVE SMOOTHIE	41
MANGO PINEAPPLE SMOOTHIE	29
MARGARITA SMOOTHIE FOR PARTY	46
PEACH GINGER SMOOTHIE	79
PEACH GREEN TEA SMOOTHIE	30
PEANUT BUTTER AND BANANA SOY MILK SMOOTHIE	65
PEANUT BUTTER BANANA PROTEIN SMOOTHIE	75
PEANUT BUTTER BANANA SMOOTHIE	27
PINEAPPLE COCONUT RELAX SMOOTHIE	43
PINEAPPLE GINGER SMOOTHIE FOR CIRCULATION	59
PINEAPPLE TURMERIC DETOX SMOOTHIE	57
PREGNANCY POWER SMOOTHIE	64
PUMPKIN AND SPICE WARM WINTER SMOOTHIE	49
QUINOA FRUIT SMOOTHIE	38
RASPBERRY WHITE CHOCOLATE SMOOTHIE	32
ROASTED RED PEPPER SMOOTHIE	38
SANGRIA SMOOTHIE FOR PARTY	46
SENIOR'S ANTI-INFLAMMATORY SMOOTHIE	52
SENIOR'S IMMUNITY-BOOSTING SMOOTHIE	52
SPINACH ARTICHOKE SMOOTHIE	36
SPINACH BERRY SMOOTHIE	30
SPINACH KALE SUPERFOOD SMOOTHIE	42
STRAWBERRY BEET ANTIOXIDANT SMOOTHIE	44

STRAWBERRY COCONUT SMOOTHIE	80
STRAWBERRY YOGURT SMOOTHIE	28
SWEET POTATO PIE SMOOTHIE FOR FALL	45
TOMATO BASIL SMOOTHIE	34
TROPICAL GREEN PROTEIN SMOOTHIE	66
TROPICAL GREEN SMOOTHIE	81
TROPICAL GREEN SMOOTHIE BOWL	67
TROPICAL TURMERIC SMOOTHIE	69
TURKEY CLUB SMOOTHIE	37
WATERMELON AND MINT SMOOTHIE	61

Made in the USA
Las Vegas, NV
27 October 2023